THE PRINCIPLES OF VIOLIN FINGERING

I. M. YAMPOLSKY

Preface by
DAVID OISTRAKH

Translated by
ALAN LUMSDEN

Music Department
OXFORD UNIVERSITY PRESS
44 CONDUIT STREET LONDON W.1

© Oxford University Press, 1967

First published 1967
Reprinted 1971

PRINTED IN GREAT BRITAIN

PREFACE

It is a pleasure for me to introduce to English readers a book devoted to violin fingering by a well-known Soviet musicologist. This book, which is the result of historical, theoretical, and practical research, embodies the artistic and methodological experience of the Soviet violin school.

Fingering is one of the most important branches of the violinist's art. The choice of the correct fingering can simplify technical difficulties and open up new artistic possibilities, but it can also have a negative effect upon the quality of his playing if the violinist has not fully considered the suitability of a particular fingering to the given technical and artistic demands of the passage.

The author examines fingering from its musical, acoustic, and physical aspects—the physiological structure of the hand, the various ways of placing and moving the fingers on the fingerboard, the demands of musical phrasing and tone colour—all of which have a direct bearing on the realization of the style of performance of a given work. He gives a clear and concise classification of fingering methods, criticizing and re-examining those in which routine and obsolete traditions prevail.

The conclusions he draws are supported by examples from violin literature given with various fingerings, a comparison of which demonstrates the advantages of the correct fingering, thus giving a practical slant to the book. Of course, one should not consider such fingering as the only one possible, but at least it gives the violinist an opportunity to reconsider his own fingering habits, and even the partial application of such rational fingerings can help to simplify certain difficulties in the given passages or in analogous cases.

One must constantly guard against the conception of fingering as an end in itself. Ease of execution is not necessarily the most important criterion in the choice of fingering, for this should always be subordinate to the musical content of the work. Often, the 'rational' fingering proves to be not better but positively worse in not producing the tone colour needed, nor giving sufficient clarity to the musical phrase. In this sense one can talk of the aesthetics of fingering, for the failure to understand the ' style ' of fingering at times destroys the musical conception of the work.

Those who love the violin and who are striving to attain mastery of their instrument should carefully study this book, for in it, in an accessible yet strictly scientific form, they will find a richness and variety of fingering devices. Every violinist should master these so as to be able to use them appropriately. This book is presented to the reader with this aim in view.

DAVID OISTRAKH

CONTENTS

		Page
Preface by David Oistrakh		iii
Foreword		v
Introduction		1
1	The Problem of Violin Fingering	18
2	Moving the Fingers on the Finger-board	21
3	Placing the Fingers on the Finger-board	25
4	The Tuning of the Violin in Fifths	28
5	Positions	32
6	Changes of Position	38
7	The Even-Numbered Positions and the Half Position	48
8	Diatonic Scales	51
9	Chromatic Scales	60
10	Broken Thirds	65
11	Arpeggios	68
12	Sevenths	71
13	Thirds	73
14	Sixths	77
15	Octaves	80
16	Mixed Types of Double-Stopping	83
17	Chords	87
18	Fingering and its Relation to Bowing	91
19	Open Strings	94
20	The Recurring Finger Pattern	99
21	Harmonics	102
22	Enharmonic Changes	115
23	Fingering and Intonation	117
24	Glissando and Portamento	119
25	Cantilena and Tone Quality	125
Conclusion		129
Index of Music Examples		130

FOREWORD

By fingering we mean both the ways of placing and moving the fingers on a musical instrument, and the means of describing this process in the music itself. Rational fingering is a vital factor in artistic violin playing—I mean by ' rational ' the most suitable way of placing and moving the fingers on the finger-board, that which allows the violinist to perform with confidence and with a minimum of effort.

The choice of fingering has to be made in relation to the demands of phrasing, dynamics, and rhythm, and is a *creative task*, dependent on the musical instincts of the performer and the intellectual and emotional content of the work to be performed—in other words, its interpretation.

The importance of fingering is shown by its effect on many varied aspects of the art of violin playing. Basically an *individual* means of artistic performance, rational fingering methods enrich the expressiveness of violin playing, allow the full possibilities of the instrument to be revealed, and help to overcome difficulties. They also develop the ability to find one's way freely about the finger-board, lead to purity of intonation and to the quick and natural mastery of the work being studied, both as a whole and in detail, strengthen the performer's musical memory, and improve sight-reading.

From this we see how necessary it is for the violinist to understand the principles of fingering and to make a serious study of the various expressive and technical possibilities which are open to him through mastery of rational fingering methods.

Despite the importance of the choice of fingering, the attention paid to this question by teachers and theorists has by no means satisfied all the demands made by classical and contemporary music. Violin methods have usually concentrated on various means of developing the fingers of the left hand and have by-passed the question of their rational use in the actual process of playing, to which they ascribe but little importance. In addition, special instruction books containing various types of exercises for the development of isolated technical points, as well as systems of gymnastic training for the fingers,[1] which were widespread from the second half of the 19th century (particularly in the German violin school), have one-sidedly fixed the attention of the violinist on the purely mechanical side of the development of technique. This could not but lead to a state of affairs in which many teachers consider work on technique as something that can easily be separated from the study of the music itself.

This lack of understanding of the true significance of fingering, of its close relation to the artistic side of performance, has in the past prevented violinists realizing the need to make a detailed study of the whole question of fingering. New methods of fingering which have appeared have not been sufficiently used in performance and have not been incorporated into a system.

The Soviet violin school, which has developed to a high degree the traditions of the pre-revolutionary school of violin playing, pays great attention to fingering disciplines. The present work is intended as both a theoretical and a practical guide. The author has endeavoured to include in it all those aspects of violin playing which are connected with fingering. The aim is, by analysing the fingering principles of the classical violin schools and of the Soviet violin school, and by criticizing other theories of fingering, to systematize rational fingering methods, to establish their relative value, and thus to give the violinist the opportunity freely to make his own individual choice of fingering.

The author has used the remarks on fingering contained in both classical and contemporary violin methods and in various editions of violin works, as well as special theoretical articles and studies devoted to this subject.

The third (Russian) edition of *The Principles of Violin Fingering* has been considerably revised and enlarged since the previous editions (1933 and 1936). The Introduction, in which the historical development of violin fingering has been considered, the chapters 'Changes of Position', 'The Even-numbered Positions and the Half Position', 'The Recurring Finger Pattern', 'Enharmonic Changes', and others have been rewritten, and considerable changes and additions have been made in the majority of the other sections.

---

[1] Like the notorious finger gymnastics of Jackson (cf. *Finger Gymnastics, with* 37 *illustrations, compiled from the works of Jackson and others,* 6th cheaper edition, Moscow, 1909). There were also in circulation numerous special appliances for the development of the fingers of the left hand.

INTRODUCTION

The history of violin fingering is as old as the art of violin playing itself. Its development is inseparably linked with the development of musical forms and ideas and with changes in musical styles. 'As almost every new musical thought has its own fingering, it follows that our present mode of thinking, which is substantially different from that of former times, has brought with it new methods of fingering,'[1] wrote C. P. E. Bach as far back as the 18th century.

The enrichment of melodic and harmonic resources and the wide spread of chromaticism, the use of the extreme high register and the new demands made on the character of instrumental sound, presented the violinist with ever greater difficulties of execution. The resolution of such problems demanded the acquisition of new modes of expression and a more finished technique, and required radical changes in the manner of holding both violin and bow, as well as the bringing to perfection of the art of violin making.

The principles and detailed technique of violin fingering have occupied the energies of many generations of musicians, and represent the crystallization of centuries of performing and teaching experience.

At first, in the 16th century, violin playing was confined to the upper three strings used in first position—the G string being used only exceptionally. The neck and finger-board were considerably shorter and wider than on the modern violin, and the manner of holding the instrument completely different, the violin being held against the left side of the chest.

The limitation of the range of the violin to the first position only was due to the immovable position of the left hand, which was used as a second point of support for the firmer holding of the instrument.

The increase of the range of notes employed with the consequent gradual development of position playing necessitated the freeing of the left hand from its immovable condition. For this to be possible a new and firmer point of support had to be established for holding the instrument, one which would allow the hand to move freely along the neck.

The violin began to be held on the shoulder, while from time to time, during changes of position, the performer would place his chin on the belly of the instrument, to the right of the tail-piece. This manner of holding the violin created the necessary conditions for the development of position playing and thus of fingering technique.

However, holding the violin to the right of the tail-piece had a fundamental disadvantage which held back the further development of violin technique. It meant that the instrument had to be held almost flat and diagonal to the body, with the left elbow inclined sharply outwards—which made playing difficult in the higher positions and on the G string—and the right elbow held well into the body, which limited the sweep of the bowing arm. This accounts for the precept, characteristic of the violin schools of the 17th and 18th centuries, that the elbow of the right arm should be kept low. For example, Campagnoli, in his *Nouvelle Méthode de la mécanique progressive du jeu de violon*, published in 1791, recommends the pupil to bind his elbow with a cord attached to the button of his coat. This low position of the right elbow, limiting the sweep of the bowing arm, explains the use of a comparatively short bow in the 17th and 18th centuries. The Italian style of holding the bow a palm's length from the nut, which was widespread at that time, made the effective length even shorter. This principle of the low position of the elbow is anachronistically retained in some teaching methods of the 19th and even of the 20th centuries.

In the opening decades of the 19th century, with the ever-increasing demands made upon performers, a new method of holding the violin established itself, with the chin placed to the left of the tail-piece. This meant a fundamental change in the position of the head, body and arms, and made it necessary to hold the violin at an angle, thus facilitating playing on the G string and in the upper positions, with the left elbow inclined inwards and the right elbow held higher and away from the body. This created the necessary conditions for developments in the use of the upper positions and the working-out of fingering techniques to cover changes of position, as well as the development of violin tone both in volume and expressiveness.

Other factors contributing to these ends were certain changes in violin construction and the fundamental reform of the bow made by Tourte in the second half of the 18th century. The short, wide neck was replaced by a longer, narrower one, set at a different angle to the body of the instrument. which made for greater freedom and lack of constriction in moving along it, The invention of the chin-rest by Spohr in 1820 freed the left hand even more from its function of holding the instrument. All this created the opportunities for the many-sided development of violin fingering and for virtuoso technique in general.[2]

This new method of holding the violin, which was completely revolutionary, only gradually won complete acceptance. Even at the beginning of the 19th century many leading violinists held the instrument in different ways : Viotti to the left of the tail-piece, Frenzl to the right, and Spohr on the tail-piece itself, to which he fixed his chin-rest.

Further final improvements in violin construction, as well as certain new aspects of playing, were dictated by the acoustic conditions of the large concert hall. The demands of volume and intensity of tone made a considerable rise in pitch necessary. This required the use of thinner and more tightly stretched strings, which, in its turn, meant that the old type of sound-post and bridge had to be replaced with new ones, capable of withstanding the increased pressure. The widespread use of vibrato, from the beginning of the 19th century onwards, was to a large extent determined by the same factors. A means not only of enhancing the expressiveness of the tone, but also of increasing its dynamic range, the use of vibrato gave to the violin that high degree of intensity which made it suitable for widespread use in the acoustic conditions of large halls.

* * * *

The earliest examples of violin fingering are shown in the form of tablature. Tablature was a system used mainly by lutenists and organists in the 15th—17th centuries, in which the music was depicted by a combination of letters, numbers, rhythmical signs, lines, etc. It was also used for violin music. Here is a characteristic example of violin numerical tablature, dating from 1613 :[3]

The four lines represent the four strings of the violin, tuned in fifths—G, D, A, E. The numbers marked on the lines (strings) represent not the pitch of the sound but the finger which should be pressed on the string to produce the required note. The lengths of the notes are depicted by special additional signs placed above the lines. This form of tablature could only be used while violin playing was confined within the limits of the first position. The development of position playing made its use impossible owing to its inordinate confusion and complexity.

Even at this early stage of the development of the art of violin playing we find isolated instances of rational fingerings, such as the careful marking—when playing a melody on two strings—to take the open string while ascending and the fourth finger descending :[4]

Galliarda

We find instances of fingering indications connected with position playing in the violin methods of the late 17th century. One of the earliest is in the German method of Merk, *A Short Treatise of Instrumental Music*, published in 1695. In this we find fingering examples up to the fourth position :[5]

In 1738 the Frenchman Corrette, in his *L'Ecole d'Orphée*, first established the exact division of the finger-board into seven positions. As the basis of this division he divided the finger-board into tones and semitones, each position covering a fourth on each string. This division, which was thenceforth adopted by the French school of violin playing, later became generally accepted :

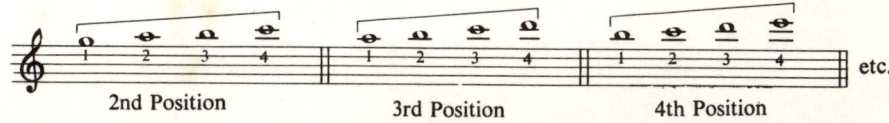

2nd Position   3rd Position   4th Position

According to Corrette, changes of position could be made on all four strings, but preferably on the E string. In the examples given, position changes on the G, D, and A strings are shown only up to the fourth position, and on the E string up to the seventh. When changing position ' it is necessary to rest the chin on the violin ; this creates the necessary freedom of the left hand, particularly when changing downward.'[6]

The Italians Locatelli and Geminiani were the first to demonstrate the possibility of using fingerings based on extensions and contractions. In his

'Capriccios' appended to the violin concertos in *The Art of the Violin* (1733), Locatelli consistently uses such extensions as an integral part of violin technique. Bearing in mind the anatomical peculiarities of the structure of the fingers he pays particular attention to first finger extensions:

In point of fact, the first finger is used for extensions far more frequently than the others, particularly the fourth finger. This is shown clearly in the technique of playing tenths. Thus it is much easier to make an extension from the fourth finger to the first than *vice versa*:

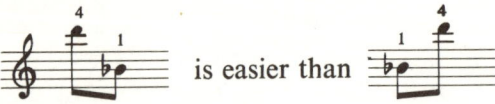

Locatelli pays no less attention to the use of the open string as a means of changing position:

These two devices played an exceptionally important role in the development of virtuoso technique.

Geminiani, in his tutor *The Art of Playing on the Violin* (1739) in which he treats of 'musical feeling and intelligence' together with aesthetic and technical matters touching on all aspects of violin playing, gave examples of various new technical devices. Thus, instead of the normal fingering for chromatic passages, based on the sliding of the fingers by semitones, Geminiani was the first to introduce a fingering in which all the fingers are used consecutively in a contracted position :[7]

Geminiani also introduced a fingering for diatonic scales based on the maximum extension of the fingers, and also on their most extreme contraction, in which the interval of a major second is taken on one string by the first and fourth fingers :[8]

This fingering given by Geminiani for position changes in a scale passage shows that he is striving for the minimum of position changes, and he recommends that no position change should be made until the possibilities of the previous position have been completely exhausted :[9]

The principles of leaving the fingers on the strings and thus preparing them are also laid down in Geminiani's book. As he states : ' It is a constant Rule to keep the Fingers as firm as possible, and not to raise them till there is a Necessity of doing it, to place them somewhere else ; and the Observance of this Rule will very much facilitate the playing of double stops.'[10]

The German violinist and pedagogue, Leopold Mozart, in his *Violin School*, published in 1756, pays detailed attention to questions of fingering, to which he devotes the whole of the eighth chapter ' On Fingering '.[11]

In this chapter Mozart for the first time gives a full definition of the proper use of fingering and positions as the most important element of the violinist's art : ' There are three reasons which justify the use of fingerings.[12] Necessity, convenience, and elegance. Necessity manifests itself when several lines are drawn over the usual five lines. Convenience requires the use of the fingerings in certain passages where the notes are set so far apart that they cannot be played otherwise without difficulty. And finally fingerings are used for the sake of elegance when notes which are Cantabile occur closely together and can be played easily on one string. Not only is equality of tone obtained thereby, but also a more consistent and singing style of delivery.'

Mozart begins his consideration of the question of fingering with the positions. In contrast to Corrette and Geminiani, he advocates a different division of the finger-board into positions which he calls ' fingerings '. Proceeding from the possibility of playing scale passages by the alternation of two pairs of adjacent fingers (1 and 2 or 2 and 3), Mozart distinguishes between *whole* and *half* ' fingerings '. A whole ' fingering ' (position) is that which produces the note A with the first finger on the E string :

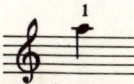

while a half fingering is when the first finger produces the note G on the E string :

Thus Mozart divides the finger-board into 1st, 2nd, 3rd, and 4th whole 'fingerings' (our present 1st, 3rd, 5th, and 7th positions) and 1st, 2nd, 3rd, and 4th half 'fingerings' (our present 2nd, 4th, 6th, and 8th positions). Moreover, these two 'fingerings' could be combined to produce what Mozart called *mixed* 'fingerings'.

This division of the finger-board was adopted by the German violin school until the 1830s. Spohr, however, considered it unnecessarily involved, and rejected it. In his *Violin School* (1832) he divides the finger-board according to the French system (p. 88).

Mozart for the first time treats systematically a number of fingering devices. He pays great attention to changes of position, emphasising the importance of making them imperceptible. To achieve this, he specifies three rational fingering methods—use of the open string, change of fingering when repeating the same note, and use of extensions.

'If, however, one is no longer constrained to remain in the position, one must not instantly run headlong down but await a good and easy opportunity to descend in such a fashion that the listener does not perceive the change. This can most conveniently be achieved if you wait for a note which can be taken on the open string, when the descent can be made quite comfortably.

'When two similar notes occur consecutively, they afford very good opportunity for descending. The first note must be taken in the upper position while the second note is played in the natural position. For example:

'After a dot, too, the descent can be made very conveniently.

'At the dot the bow is lifted, during which the hand is moved and the note F taken in the natural position.'

In order to avoid excessive changes of position, Mozart recommends the use of fourth finger extensions, and also allows the extension of the second finger:

He also recommends the same method for certain types of double-stopping:

In slow cantabile pieces a combination of fourth finger extensions and glissandi can be used to intensify the expressiveness of the performance and to maintain homogeneity of timbre throughout a musical phrase:

'In slow pieces the fourth finger is often used, not from necessity but for the sake of equality of tone and therefore also for the sake of elegance. For example:

The minim F could, it is true, be taken on the E string, with the first finger. But as the E string sounds far too shrill against the A string, the tone is made more level if the F is taken indeed with the fourth finger but without the hand changing its position, and the note E is also taken with the fourth finger. Indeed, the passage hangs better together and is rendered thereby more melodious.'

Mozart also points out the necessity of coordinating the fingering with the bowing and recommends different fingerings for one and the same passage depending on the bowing used:

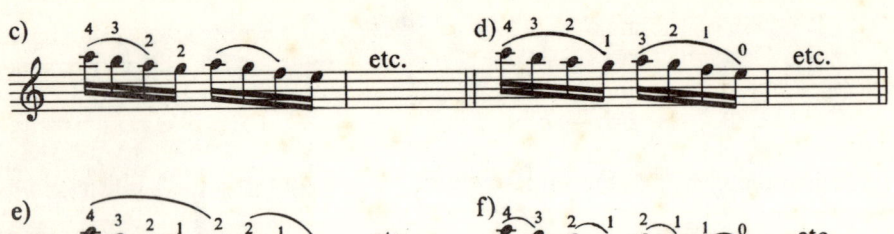

The Frenchman, L'Abbé, in his method *Les Principes du violon*, published in 1761, was the first to make use of the *half-position*. Using the scale of G sharp minor as an example, he explains that to use the fingering marked ' it is necessary to bring the hand closer to the nut ' : [11]

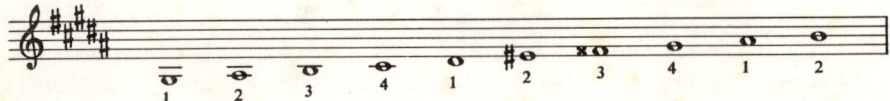

He demonstrates the logic of using the half position in both major and minor sharp keys, which allows certain passages to be played without changing the position of the hand :

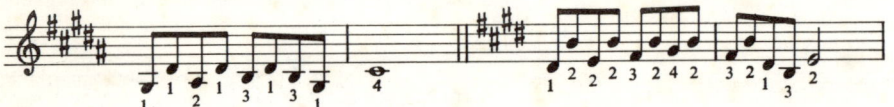

L'Abbé shows different ways of playing perfect and diminished fifths on two strings. The first has the same finger placed on both strings simultaneously :

The second uses two adjacent fingers :

The Russian violinist Khandoshkin in his *Russian Songs with Variations* for violin and bass, published in the last quarter of the 18th century, was the first to use the virtuoso technique of playing on one string only (the G string). This technique is based not on the principle of exhausting all possible finger movements within any one given fixed hand position, but on the opposite principle—that of the maximum use of *position changes*. By introducing the use of the G string throughout its compass, Khandoshkin laid down a new and most important principle of fingering, based on the dynamic mobility of the hand. Later, this principle was widely used by the violinists of the 19th century (Paganini, Ernst, and others).

It was by adopting this violin technique of playing on one string that Davydov revolutionized cello fingering. V. P. Gutor, in his book on Davydov's playing and teaching methods, comments on the use of the device of playing on one string, rightly pointing out that the resultant frequent changes of position produce a more expressive and technically more finished execution. 'The habit of using movements of the whole hand makes for strength and accuracy of finger placing; a phrase played on one string with a change of position sounds more finished than when played in the same position, when the notes of a single phrase are spread over two or even three strings of different timbres. In this sense the practice of using the greatest possible movement of the hand can be considered *the basic principle of the most advanced instrumental virtuosity*.'[14]

Below are some characteristic examples of this use of the G string (the so-called sopra una corda) from the *Russian Songs with Variations* for violin and bass of Khandoshkin:[15]

Thus, in the 18th century, within the confines of the classical school of violin playing, all the basic principles of rational fingering were already established, and the most important technical devices already worked out. Most of these, however, did not receive general acceptance until much later. At this period the theory of fingering outstripped the practice of violin playing, which was bound by traditional rules and limited mainly to chamber music performance.

In the 19th century, with the vast development of virtuoso violin technique and with the appearance of an immense corpus of concerto literature for the violin, a new stage begins in the development of both the theory and practice of fingering. In this Paganini played an enormous role, as both composer and executant. This is natural. The innovations of Paganini, with his own particular virtuoso techniques, required the introduction of new methods of fingering. Many of these, being connected with the individual peculiarities of his style of execution, may appear at the present time somewhat unusual and, to a certain extent, as having lost their value. But the historical significance of the fingering innovations of Paganini is extremely great, for by them he broke through the bounds of the classical school of the 18th century, which were a barrier against the introduction of new principles into performing practice.

Adopting and developing in his works the principles of Locatelli, based on finger extensions and wide stretches, Paganini dispensed with the concept of positions and thus opened up limitless possibilities for the development of fingering technique.

The originality of Paganini's fingering, which ignored the dogmas of the schools, did not remain unnoticed by his contemporaries. 'Paganini's fingering, which is occasionally incorrect or, rather, free from any fingering rules, is not the result of caprice but of a deep and well thought-out method.'[15] 'Paganini played chords and arpeggios of enormous difficulty and generally used a completely individual method of fingering.'[17] 'His fingering technique in no way resembles that taught in the schools.'[18]

Much valuable information about Paganini's fingering is contained in Guhr's book *Paganini's Art of Playing the Violin*, published in 1829. In the chapter 'Paganini's works for one string and their performance' Guhr shows that the most important stage in developing mastery of playing on one string is the development of a complete scale technique. In the very high positions Paganini played scale passages with one finger, says Guhr, and appends the following example of such fingering:

In the chapter 'The highest difficulties of Paganini', Guhr gives examples of extensions used by Paganini, and recommends the following fingerings:

The fingering used by Paganini in passages of tenths is interesting:

Striving for the utmost possible continuity and cantabile in cantilena passages, Paganini often used one finger, or, for double stops, one pair of fingers. The fingering he uses in the Capriccio No. 21 is instructive in this respect:

Paganini, *Capriccio No. 21*

In the 18th century the basic sources of information about violin fingering are the methods and tutors for the instrument. In violin pieces published at the time marks connected with performance, including fingering indications, occur only rarely.

In the 19th century a vast amount of material for the study of violin fingering and its connection with various styles of performance is to be found not only in methods and tutors but also in editions and transcriptions made by leading violinists. The editions and transcriptions made by Ernst, Joachim, David, Léonard, and later by Kreisler and other violinists contain a large number of performing indications, particularly as regards fingering. The transcription, which served not only to widen the violin repertoire, but also to enrich the resources of violin technique, had an important influence on the development of new fingering devices.

Each violinist's editions and transcriptions reflected his own peculiarities of style and execution, which accounts for the abundance of performing indications.

The widening and enriching of violin technique in the 19th century found its expression most of all in the colossal development of double stopping and chord playing. This was due to the influence of Paganini's playing, which had an enormous effect in bringing new rational fingerings for double stops and chords—an aspect of technique scarcely touched upon in the methods of the 18th century—into the realms of normal violin technique.[19]

In this connection mention should be made of Ferdinand David's edition of the Bach Sonatas and Partitas for violin solo, published in 1843, in which new fingerings for four-part chords making use of contractions are given; Wilhelmj's cadenza to the first movement of Paganini's D major violin concerto, in which he uses for the first time a new fingering for octaves, based on extensions of the 1st and 3rd, and 2nd and 4th fingers, which led to the development of a new kind of technique for double-stopping—the so-called 'fingered octaves'; and Léonard's *La Gymnastique du violoniste* in which new fingerings for sixths are given, based on a completely new principle—the extreme contraction of the fingers.

In 1859 A. F. Lvov gave examples of rational fingerings for descending broken thirds, based not on sliding the same finger, but on the extension of two adjacent fingers, which ensures an imperceptible change of position.[20] In the 1870s F. Zhigardlovich mentioned the need for the violinist to master the various ways of placing the fingers on the finger-board to ensure the free use of various fingering devices.[21] Analysing the methods used by the greatest violin virtuosi in playing three and four octave scales he systematized a number of rational fingerings used by them.

The *Method* by Ch. Bériot contains some important principles of violin fingering. In this work the significance of fingering as an individual means of artistic expression is established for the first time. 'We can divide violin fingerings into two kinds', writes Bériot, 'one for expression and one for technique, or, in other words, one for cantabile melodies and one for fast passage-work. The fingering used by different virtuosi in melodic passages is an important means of expression ; it is used for binding the sounds together and for imitating the inflexions of the human voice. It varies from performer to performer according to the sentiment he wishes to express . . . That which we call passage-work fingering has as its object the ability to play the passage with the greatest possible facility and evenness. As this fingering, with which we will concern ourselves first of all in this article, is not subject, as is melodic fingering, to diversity of taste, it can be brought within certain rules.'[22]

Bériot suggested that teaching should begin not with the scale of C major, as in the old methods, but with the scale of G major. In this way he emphasized the necessity of starting instruction by using the natural disposition of the fingers on the finger-board, as is needed for this scale, a fact which later played an important part in the establishment of this disposition of the fingers as the basis of violin fingering. Bériot also developed a new fingering for chromatic scales, based not on one finger moving by semitones, but on the use of all the fingers in succession, which was one of the most significant steps forward in the development of violin technique. He also had many important things to say regarding the working-out of rational fingerings for diatonic scales.

The first half of the 19th century saw the first attempts to summarize and define the concept of rational fingering. One of the first such definitions was given in 1835 by the Russian musical scholar and critic M. P. Rezvoi in his article ' Fingering '. This contains a clear and concise definition of fingering, and stresses the importance of the performer studying *correct* (i.e. rational) fingering. ' In music, fingering is the method and order of using the fingers when playing stringed instruments. It is essential for the musician to learn good fingering, as it is largely and often almost entirely on this that purity of intonation and tone depend. The correct use of the fingers is that which allows the artist to perform works written for stringed instruments with certainty and the minimum of difficulty. But as several different paths often lead to the same spot, so one meets in music passages which allow the use of different fingerings, each as good as the other. There are, however, certain basic rules from which one should not diverge.'[23]

The last quarter of the 19th century saw the beginnings of the appearance of special theoretical works devoted to the problem of violin fingering. Among these we should mention the brief work of the German C. Wassmann[24] in which the author for the first time points out the possibilities inherent in the violin's tuning in fifths and the significance of the perfect fifth between two strings taken by the same finger as a *point of support* for the fingers in any given position. Developing this idea, Wassmann suggests a uniform scheme of fingering for all diatonic and chromatic scales, giving maximum economy of position changes (for an example, see the chapter ' Scales '). The main defect of Wassmann's work is that he considers the problems of fingering from a purely technical point of view, without reference to the artistic side of performance.

Many pre-revolutionary Russian writers such as Valter, Bezekirsky, Lessmann, Dulov, and Nazarov made valuable contributions to the problems of finding rational systems of fingering. Valter lays stress on the importance of using the even-numbered positions, particularly the second, and points out that their avoidance leads to the violinist ' being unable to choose the correct fingering '.[25] Bezekirsky is one of the first to give examples of rational fingerings for various kinds of double-stops, based on the use of extensions and the simultaneous use of two adjacent positions.[26] Lessmann, whose book is devoted to an examination of the teaching methods of L. S. Auer, which he characterizes as being 'a school of artistic playing', pays particular attention to the importance of using what is sometimes called 'rhythmic fingering' when making quick position changes.[27] Dulov gives rational fingerings for so-called 'Fingersatzen' in scale-like passages, facilitating their execution in fast tempi.[28] Nazarov stresses the importance of studying scales in a number of different fingerings.[29]

Among modern Western writers, the most important contributions to the subject are the *New Theory of Fingering. Paganini and his Secret* of A. Jarosy (Paris, 1922), and the relevant section in Carl Flesch's *The Art of Violin Playing* (Berlin, 1922).

Jarosy developed in his book the idea formulated by Wassmann concerning the significance of the perfect fifth between two strings taken by the same finger, not only as a *point of support*, but as an *axis* round which the other fingers can freely move. In this way Jarosy revealed the underlying principle of many fingering devices used by modern violinists. At the same time, Jarosy's work has the basic fault of not considering the artistic side of playing as an integral part of technique. He gives an arbitrary definition of the natural disposition of the fingers on one string as that in which the first and fourth fingers define between them a major third or diminished fourth. The natural distance between the fingers, according to Jarosy, is a tone between the first and second fingers, a semitone between the second and third and a semitone between the third and fourth. The whole tone between the second and third fingers is considered by Jarosy as an extension, and he recommends in such cases the use of the second and fourth fingers (leaving out the third). Thus he replaces what is in fact the natural disposition of the fingers, which gives a perfect fourth between the first and fourth fingers, by a contracted one giving a major third or diminished fourth. And from this contrived system of 'natural' fingering, which he pretentiously links with the 'secret' of Paganini, Jarosy gives in the majority of cases fingerings which are purely speculative and of little practical application, and which are moreover divorced from real music and detrimental to the tone quality of the instrument.

The chapter on fingering in Flesch's work is of considerably more practical value. In it the author systematically analyses the various finger movements and fingering conventions. As opposed to Jarosy, Flesch goes into the question of the choice of fingering in relation to artistic demands. At the same time, his psychological over-refinement, a tendency to excessive detail in phrasing leading to a segmented view of the whole work, the self-contained and restricted meaning given to the concept of the 'beautiful tone', an over-refinement and artificiality resulting from a striving for complex gradations in tone colour—all this leads to a lack of simplicity, which considerably reduces the value of Flesch's fingerings in his editions of the Beethoven Concerto, the Solo Sonatas and Partitas of Bach and other works.

The Soviet violin school considers fingering first of all as one of many artistic means leading to the correct interpretation of the contents of a musical work. At the same time, teachers pay particular attention to the use of rational fingering as a means of overcoming difficulties and thus of achieving complete mastery of the instrument. Of considerable significance in this connection is the work carried out in the violin classes of the Moscow Conservatoire, started in the 1920s by Professor L. M. Zeitlin and continued by Professors A. I. Yampolsky, K. G. Mostras and D. F. Oistrakh, of bringing into violin playing a number of new rational fingering techniques. In the editions of A. I. Yampolsky (the concertos of Mendelssohn and Bach and the studies of Kreutzer), D. F. Oistrakh (the concertos of Rakov, Saint-Saëns, Khachaturian, and Kabalevsky and the Prokofiev Sonata No. 1 for violin and piano), K. G. Mostras (editions, arrangements, transcriptions, and original pieces) are a number of new rational fingering devices, individually chosen to serve the ends of artistic interpretation.

In the early 1930s there began to appear various theoretical works by Soviet pedagogues devoted to fingering questions—the article by M. G. Plaksin, ' Extreme contraction as a new device in violin technique ', and the first edition of the present work. In his article, Plaksin draws attention to the insufficient use of contracted fingerings—one of the most important devices in rational fingering. Using the most extreme contraction between all the fingers—a semitone between the first and third and even between the first and fourth fingers—Plaksin built up an entirely new system of fingering.

As Plaksin points out, the principles developed by him in his article ' do not in any way attempt to change existing violin technical methods, but rather to broaden and add to them.'[30]

In establishing the principle of extreme contraction, Plaksin starts with the premise that while the principle of finger extensions was carried to its furthest limits by Paganini, ' its converse, the extreme contraction of the fingers, was not used at all '. Moreover, Plaksin points out, ' it is sufficient to look at any hand to convince oneself that the contracted disposition of the fingers presents no difficulty, while the conventional position of the hand on the finger-board necessitates a certain strain. I maintain that this is sufficient evidence of the naturalness of such a fingering.' ' Exercising the fingers in this way will doubtless lead to the development and perfection of the technique as a whole.'

The use of the fingering methods advocated by Plaksin makes it possible to play successions of intervals and chords which are in the majority of cases unplayable using conventional fingerings. This, suggests Plaksin, ' will serve as an enrichment of the resources available to future composers for solo and chamber music.'

According to Plaksin, the basic uses of the new method of extreme contraction are the following. He suggests a new fingering for diatonic scales :

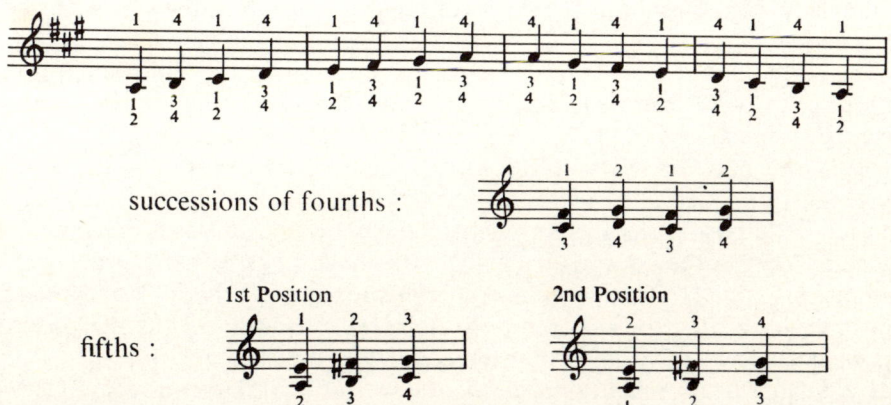

sixths:

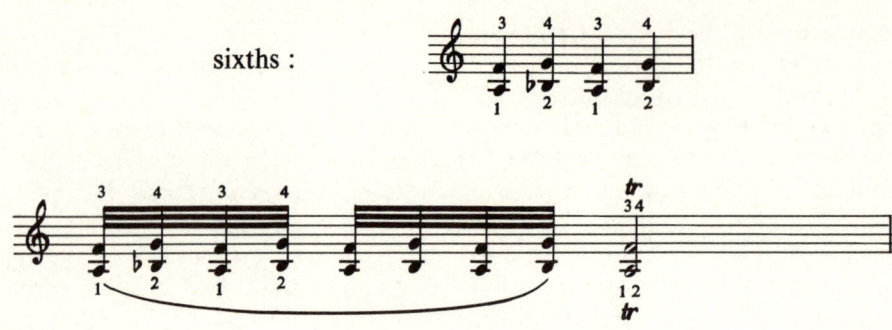

various kinds of chord progressions:

and also a fingering for trills, based on the use of all the fingers in alternation:

While recognizing the importance of Plaksin's system of fingering, it must be pointed out that neither classical nor modern violin music requires so wide a use of extreme contraction. (In attempting to remedy this deficiency in the violin repertoire, Plaksin has written whole pieces based on his system, music constructed entirely of successions of seconds, fourths, sevenths, and so on.) There is no doubt that the widespread use of extreme contraction to a large extent destroys the natural sound of the violin and makes pure intonation difficult to achieve. This leads one to the conclusion that it should only *occasionally* be used in practical performance.

An unquestionably rational fingering device suggested by Plaksin, however, is the changing of position by means of contraction rather than with the help of a slide.

There are certain interesting observations concerning the choice of rational fingerings in A. M. Veksler's *Certain acoustic phenomena on the violin and their expressive significance.*[31]

From the point of view of the further development of rational fingering, D. F. Oistrakh's concept of the zones of positions is extremely fruitful: he considers the position not as an unchanging static unit but as a dynamic one, changing during the course of playing. In modern performing practice, the violinist often has to choose a fingering which is outside the normal limit of a fourth contained in the one position, or even of a fifth. Thus the position can be considered as being within the zone of a fourth to a fifth.

The further development of such theories of rational fingering will doubtless improve still more the technical mastery of the violin.

FOOTNOTES TO INTRODUCTION.

[1] *Versuch über die wahre Art das Klavier zu spielen* (1753).
[2] About the same time (from the second half of the 18th century) begins the development of virtuoso technique on the cello, due to the introduction of new fingering methods, in particular the use of the *thumb position*.
[3] Quoted from E. van der Straeten, *The History of the Violin*, vol. I (Kassel, 1933), p. 37.
[4] Quoted from A. Moser, *Geschichte des Violinspiels* (Berlin, 1923), p. 63.
[5] Quoted from G. Beckmann, *Das Violinspiel in Deutschland vor 1700* (Leipzig, 1918), p. 41.
[6] Quoted from Lionel de la Laurencie, *L'école française de Violin de Lully à Viotti* (Paris, 1924), t.III, p. 17.
[7] op. cit., p. 27.
[8] loc. cit.
[9] op. cit., p. 28.
[10] op. cit., p. 26.
[11] English translation (O.U.P., 2nd ed. 1951), pp. 132–65.
[12] Used in the sense of ' positions '. See below.
[13] L. de la Laurencie, op. cit., p. 52.
[14] V. P. Gutor, *K. Y. Davydov as the founder of a school* (Moscow/Leningrad, 1950), p. 13.
[15] I. Yampolsky, *Russian Violin Playing*, vol. I (Moscow/Leningrad, 1951), pp. 410, 436.
[16] G. J. de Laphalèque, *Notice sur le célèbre violiniste N. Paganini* (Paris, 1830).
[17] J. M. Schottky, *Paganini's Leben und Treiben* (Prague, 1830).
[18] F. Fétis, *N. Paganini, Notice Biographique* (Paris, 1851).
[19] Despite the fact that the technique of double-stopping had almost from the beginning of violin playing attracted the attention of performers, in the middle of the 18th century it was still an unresolved problem in both the theory and practice of violin playing. There were even some who rejected double-stopping altogether. Thus the English musician Avison writes in 1753 : ' even in the hands of the greatest masters double-stopping destroys sonority, makes the expression false and slows up execution . . . and brings one good instrument down to the level of two pale reflections.'
[20] *Advice to beginners on playing the violin* by A. F. Lvov, with 24 musical examples (Saint Petersburg, 1859), Caprice No. 3.
[21] *Instructions for the development of the mechanism of violin playing. Compiled according to the methods of the famous violinist F. Zhigardlovich* (Moscow, P. Jurgenson), p. 1.
[22] Ch. Bériot, *Méthode de violon en trois parties* (1858). Bériot develops the principles of the division of fingerings laid down by Baillot, who distinguishes three basic types of fingering (1) the most generally reliable fingering, (2) the simplest fingering for those with small hands (3) the most expressive fingering for bringing out the characteristic style of different compositions (P. Baillot, *L'Art du violon, Nouvelle Méthode* (Mayence, 1834).
[23] *Encyclopaedic Lexicon*, vol. I, A–ALM (Saint Petersburg, 1835), the so-called Pluchard Lexicon.
[24] C. Wassmann, *Entdeckungen zur Erleichterung und Erweiterung Violintechnik durch selbstständige Ausbildung des Tastgefühls der Finger* (Berlin, 1885).
[25] *How to learn to play the violin* (Saint Petersburg, 1897).
[26] *A short historical survey of violin playing in the 17th and 18th centuries* (Kiev, 1913), p. 40.
[27] *Violin technique and its development in the school of Professor L. S. Auer* (Saint Petersburg, 1909).
[28] *A systematic course of scales*, part II, p. 4.
[29] *The essence and basis of musical technique*, 2nd ed.
[30] M. Plaksin, ' Contracted fingering as a new device in violin technique ' (*Soviet Music*, 1933, No. 2).
[31] Ph.D. thesis. MS, 1949, library of the Tchaikovsky State Conservatoire, Moscow.

CHAPTER I

THE PROBLEM OF VIOLIN FINGERING

For any given succession of notes there is an inherently rational fingering. In practice, however, violinists will often use different fingerings. The reasons for this variety are basically :

(*a*) principles of performance and technical methods common to a particular school ;

(*b*) the individual interpretation of this or that musical composition by the artist ;

(*c*) anatomical peculiarities of the performer in the build of the shoulder, hand and fingers.

The first case is well illustrated by the fact that those violinists who use a strong pressure of the fingers on the strings and a similar strong hold on the neck of the violin (which makes changes of position comparatively difficult) prefer, often to the detriment of the sound, that fingering which allows them to keep the hand still and not move from one position to another (a peculiarity, for example, of violinists of the German school).

A good example of the second case is the fingering of Kreisler, which is indissolubly linked with the general style of his playing, and which outside that style to a large extent loses its raison d'être.

Anatomical peculiarities in the build of the shoulder, hand, and fingers have a great influence on the choice of fingering.[1] Violinists' hands vary considerably in size and their fingers in length, thickness, and span. These differences influence their choice of fingering.

However, unduly short or thick fingers, small finger span and excessively narrow hands are exceptional. In such cases one must adapt one's whole technique to one's own hand and finger formation. But for the majority of violinists, differences in fingering result solely from the casual way in which fingerings are selected.

All this does not prove that general rules governing the choice of fingering do not exist. At the basis of the selection of fingerings, as indeed of bowings and phrasings, are certain objective principles, based on the laws of musical logic. These should be maintained, although they can of course be interpreted and modified in different ways by different individuals.

The basis for the selection of a rational fingering is the organic reciprocity of the following elements :

(*a*) the nature of the instrument ;
(*b*) the disposition of fingers on finger-board which this requires ;
(*c*) the texture of the musical composition.

In some cases the disposition of the fingers on the finger-board required by the nature of the instrument and the texture of the musical composition are mutually contradictory, which creates for the performer what are known as ' technically awkward ' passages. These cases are met with fairly frequently, as composers writing for this or that solo instrument are often not fully aware of its technical capabilities.

This accounts for the widespread existence of numerous different performing editions of one and the same work, sometimes substantially different from the composer's original, which has been adapted to suit the technical possibilities of the instrument or the individual peculiarities of the editor's playing.

Often, composers write works in collaboration with leading performers. Thus, for example, the Mendelssohn Concerto was written in collaboration with the eminent German violinist David, the Brahms with Joachim, the 2nd Concerto of Szymanowski with Kochanski. This had a great influence on the character of the solo writing of these works. Some works were written taking into account the special capabilities of this or that leading artist. Thus Lalo's *Symphonie Espagnole*, and Saint-Saëns' 3rd Concerto, *Introduction and Rondo Capriccioso*, and *Havanaise* were written specially for Sarasate. The famous Spanish violinist had small hands, could scarcely stretch an octave and practically never used double-stopping. This explains the preponderance in these works of fine ' pearly ' passage-work, for which Sarasate was so famous.

The different natures of the various string instruments determines not only what fingering can be used, but also how important a role fingering plays. On the violin a change of fingering for one and the same note usually implies a significant change in its timbre and strength, independently of the way in which the finger is put down or the use of the bow. This is because the same note may be taken on different strings :

and the change in the strength and timbre of the note in this instance depends primarily on the thickness and quality of the strings which produce the sound. In addition, one and the same note may be produced on various strings *with the same fingering* :

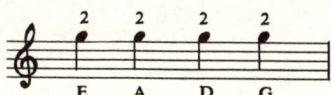

Thus the significance of fingering in violin playing, and its influence on the timbre and colour of one and the same note, is greater than, for example, in piano playing. In piano playing, a change in fingering on the same note results in no significant change in its strength and timbre, which depends to a large extent on the quality and strength of depression, the individual character of the pianist's touch, pedalling and so forth. We are not yet considering the fact that the violinist's purity of intonation often depends on the fingering used, but this problem also does not confront the pianist, for whom the pitch is already fixed.

As to the violin and the cello, the difference in fingering methods on these two related instruments is obviously determined by their difference in size. On the cello, with the same number of strings tuned in fifths, the fingering 1, 2, 4 and 1, 3, 4 (in other words, with the omission of adjacent fingers), is explained by the difficulty of extending the fingers on a larger instrument. The technique of using all five fingers of the left hand in cello playing (the so-called thumb position) could be developed on the cello owing to the way in which the instrument is held, which allows the thumb to be freed from its function of holding the instrument, but this is not possible on the violin.

While fingering possibilities are determined by the above-mentioned factors inherent in the nature of the instrument, the basis of the choice of fingering is dependent on the musical nature of the work to be performed. The realization of the wide artistic significance of fingering and its organic link with various aspects of performance, thus raising it to its rightful place in the art of violin playing—this is one of the most important tasks of the violin pedagogue.

[1] See B. A. Struve's *Typical hand positions of instrumentalists. The string section* (Moscow, 1932).

CHAPTER II

MOVING THE FINGERS ON THE FINGER-BOARD

Playing the violin demands a high degree of independence of the fingers of the left hand, and their exact coordination both with the player's auditory impressions and with the movements of the bowing arm. The peculiar difficulty of violin technique (as opposed to piano technique, for example) consists in the entirely different functions and movements of the left and right hands. Violin playing in fact exemplifies the amazing subtlety of movement attained by the human hand.

Even playing the first position, movements of the wrist and elbow are involved, as well as of the fingers of the left hand. Playing in more than one position requires a high degree of coordination of fingers, wrist, and elbow.

Basically, these movements can be grouped into four types:

(1) The *vertical* or *falling* movement of placing the 1st, 2nd, 3rd, and 4th fingers and taking them off again. This is used for both ascending and descending successions of intervals in one position and on one string:

(2) The *horizontal* or *lateral* movement of the fingers along the finger-board: their extension, sliding, the movement of the hand along the neck of the violin while changing position. This is used for chromatics and for finger extensions. The movement of the thumb when moving from one position to the next can also be classed under this heading:

(3) The movement of the fingers *across* the finger-board (right to left and back again): moving a finger to the next string or across more than one string, or more than one finger in the case of chords:[1]

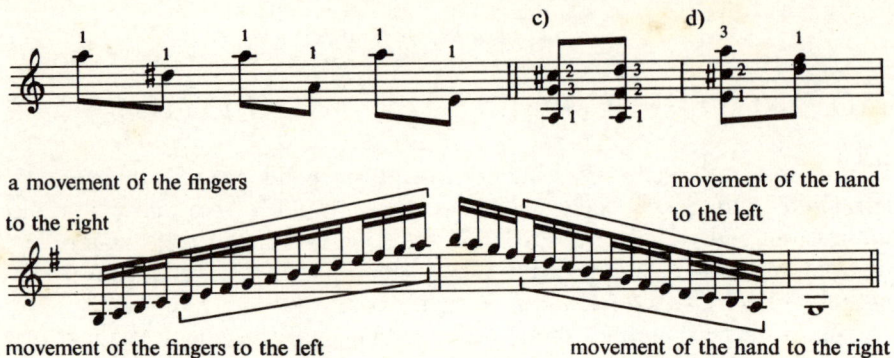

(4) The *combined* movement of the fingers, wrist, and elbow when moving from one position to another. In this case all the above-mentioned movements of the fingers are possible :

In choosing a fingering, the violinist is limited to what can be done within these basic types of finger movement, either singly or combined.

The technique of double-stopping, which includes all the types of movement enumerated above, often in complex combination, consists in the simultaneous movement of two fingers on two adjacent strings. These simultaneous movements can be divided into : (1) conjunct, (2) partially conjunct, (3) contrary.

(1) *Conjunct* movement is the simultaneous movement of two fingers in the same direction while maintaining exactly the same interval between them. Its use includes octaves and all kinds of chromatics :

(2) *Partially conjunct* movement is the simultaneous movement of two fingers in the same direction while maintaining a similar, but not identical, interval between them, e.g., in its simple form the playing of thirds and tenths :

In its compound form (with fingers crossing strings) it is used for the playing of fourths and sixths :

In such cases everyone knows the feeling of awkwardness in successions of fourths or sixths, caused by the same finger crossing strings and resulting in the interval of a perfect, augmented, or diminished fifth with the lower note of the second sixth or fourth :

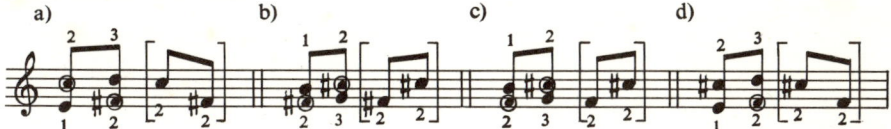

(3) *Contrary* movement is the *simultaneous* movement of two fingers *in different directions*:

Not all combinations of these various movements result in a convenient and rational fingering. Among such irrational fingerings we must class :

(1) Moving one finger several times in succession, particularly when moving a whole tone (in fast tempi) :

(2) Crossing strings with the same finger, particularly in legato playing :

(3) Simultaneously moving two fingers in different directions along the finger-board :

The use of *bad* and *inconvenient* fingerings results in an excess of unnatural movements of the left hand. It follows that the best fingering ensures the most convenient disposition of the fingers on the finger-board for any given passage in any given position.

[1] The gradual movement of the left arm to the left when playing ascending passages in first position, and to the right in descending passages, has an important significance in violin technique. The first to draw attention to this movement was the Rumanian violinist and teacher I. Voiku, who called it a steering movement. (I. Voiku, *The development of a natural system of violin playing. The technique of the left hand*. Translated from the German by V. N. Rimsky-Korsakov (Moscow, 1930), Chapter XV, ' Playing on all four strings.')

CHAPTER III

PLACING THE FINGERS ON THE FINGER-BOARD

As well as the various ways of *moving* the fingers considered in the previous chapter there are various ways of *placing* them on the finger-board. In fact there are three ways: the *natural*, the *contracted*, and the *extended*, and these form the basis of all the various principles of violin fingering.

The natural position of the fingers. If one holds the violin correctly and lets the fingers fall freely on the strings, the 1st and 2nd fingers fall somewhat obliquely in relation to the neck, while the 3rd and 4th point in a line which intersects the imaginary continuation of the line described by the first two fingers.[1]

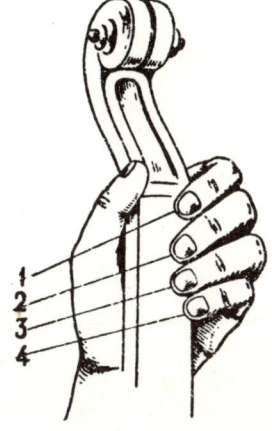

With the fingers thus falling freely, the following intervals are produced: a whole tone between the 1st and 2nd fingers, a semitone between the 2nd and 3rd, and a whole tone between the 3rd and 4th. For example:

This disposition of the fingers, which describes a perfect fourth between the 1st and 4th fingers, is the *natural* position of the fingers, and is the basis of violin fingering.

One of the main difficulties in playing the violin lies in the contradiction which often occurs between the natural position of the fingers and the position of the fingers required by the music. A good deal of the beginner violinist's daily practice is devoted to overcoming this difficulty.

Joachim was the first to point out the reason for these difficulties.[2] He considered that one of the basic mistakes of the earlier schools of violin playing was that they started with the scale of C major. The choice of this key as the basis for elementary instruction on the violin showed, according to Joachim, a lack of attention to the nature of the instrument, as correct intonation in the scale of C major in the first position presents considerable difficulties to the beginner, requiring an unnatural disposition of the fingers of the left hand (the semitone between the first and second fingers):

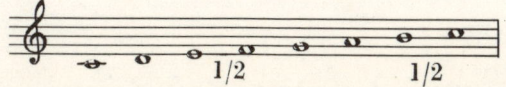

In laying down the principle that instruction should start with the scale of D major, Joachim pointed out that he was only developing the idea of Bériot, who was the first to take this difficulty into account, and who suggested in his *Violin Method* that instruction should start with the scale of G major. The disposition of the fingers in this scale played in the first position is more natural than in the scale of C major :

The scale of D major (which requires the same disposition of the fingers as the scale of G major) is more suitable still as the basis for elementary instruction on the violin, since it provides a more convenient starting point for the correct positioning of the left elbow and also for bowing :

Most of the cases of faulty intonation that one comes across in beginners are the result of placing the fingers on the finger-board in the position Joachim considered unnatural. Only gradually, in the course of practice, do the fingers accustom themselves to their correct positioning on the finger-board. Moreover, these difficulties, being the result of the particular anatomical structure of the fingers, are not always completely overcome, and make themselves felt even with more advanced violinists.

The natural tendency of the third finger to place itself a semitone from the second is an obstacle which has to be overcome every time it needs to be placed at a wider interval :

To the same type of unnaturalness belongs the greater difficulty of moving the first finger back :

and the fourth finger up :

The contracted position of the fingers. It is often necessary in the course of playing for the natural position, with a perfect fourth between the 1st and 4th fingers, to be replaced by a contracted position, with a diminished fourth or a minor third :

The following types of contracted fingering are used :

The extended position of the fingers. The natural position, describing a perfect fourth between the 1st and 4th fingers, can be extended to an augmented fourth or perfect fifth (in the lower register) :

and to a sixth or seventh (in the upper register) :

This type of disposition of the fingers is usually known simply as an extension :

Contractions and extensions are : (a) one of the most important resources of fingering combinations, (b) an aid to imperceptible position changes.

[1] I. Voiku, op. cit., p. 23.
[2] I. Joachim und A. Moser, *Violinschule* (Berlin, 1905), Erste Theil, s. 8.

CHAPTER IV

THE TUNING OF THE VIOLIN IN FIFTHS

The violin in the form in which we know it today is the result of centuries of development and change in the construction of string instruments. From the point of view of the examination of violin fingering, changes in the construction of string instruments, the number of strings and their tuning, are of great interest.

The predecessor of the violin in fashionable taste was the viol. This instrument, with its low-tensioned strings tuned in fourths and one third, with its wide fretted finger-board, and with a lower bridge than the violin, met the artistic requirements of polyphonic playing, as it facilitated double-stopping and chord playing. The tuning of instruments of the viol type, however, restricted the compass and made for a fingering system in which the 4th finger, and sometimes the 3rd as well, were rarely used, whereas the fifths of the violin extended the range of stringed instruments and required the use of all four fingers.

If one retunes the violin in fourths with one third, one can see that the compass is considerably reduced, the playing of triads and other combinations of notes brought into practice by the homophonic style is made more difficult, and the sound of the instrument becomes duller:

The limitation of compass when strings are tuned in fourths with one third explains the numerous strings which instruments with such a tuning had, as adding extra strings brought about a certain increase in range.

A change in the tuning of the violin (the so-called scordatura) was occasionally used by composers and performers, starting in the 17th century, with the aim of achieving a particular tone-quality or of making certain combinations of chords possible which would be unplayable on an instrument tuned in fifths (e.g. the unaccompanied Sonatas of Biber, certain Sonatas of Tartini, Nardini, Lulli). The changes in tuning used by Paganini are not strictly speaking scordatura. He either retuned just the G string, on which he then played the whole piece, or raised all the strings a semitone to produce greater brightness and intensity of tone. In modern music too changes in tuning are sometimes used, both in solo and orchestral works. Such changes in tuning making playing much more difficult, as they require unusual methods of fingering.

The tuning of the violin in perfect fifths, and the use of all four fingers in playing, meant that the whole technique of the left hand, all movements of the fingers on the finger-board, were based on the tetrachord. (The technical and fingering difficulties which came into violin playing with the wide use of chromaticism in post-classical music illustrate the inherent antagonism between a basically *diatonic* instrument, which the violin is, and the growing *chromatic* nature of modern music.)

We can note the following advantages of the fifth tuning of the violin, which makes possible :

(a) a complete range of over two octaves, without changing position (impossible with any other tuning) ;

(b) the playing of triads with practically no movement in the left hand, which is facilitated by the abundance of open strings in fifths :

(c) the use of the interval of the perfect fifth made by the first finger on two adjacent strings as a *point of support* for the other fingers in a given position :

The perfect fifth formed by one finger on two adjacent strings is only fully justified in fingering combinations when it is *not merely a point of support, but acts at the same time as an axis*, around which the other fingers can move easily and freely on the various strings :

Beethoven, *Sonata No. 7*, 1st Mvt.

Point of support and axis.

A single finger on one string may also serve as a point of support and axis. In such cases the fifth is implied :

Viotti, *Concerto No. 23*, 1st Mvt.

Implied point of support and axis.

The awkwardness in playing such passages with normal fingerings is caused in the majority of cases by the incomplete use of the fifth, which is considered as a point of support only, and rarely as an axis. For example :

Brahms. *Concerto*, 3rd Mvt.
Allegro giocoso ma non troppo vivace

In this example, the awkwardness is caused by the crossing of the first finger at the interval of a diminished fifth in a fast tempo:

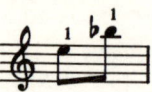

This difficulty is explained by the fact that the relationship of the notes:

which becomes by enharmonic change a perfect fifth and is used as a point of support, is not used at the same time as an axis around which the other fingers could move with greater ease and freedom. The fingering normally used, as shown above, in which the first finger crosses from one string to the next at an interval of a diminished fifth, makes it necessary to change the point of support several times from one string to another, which leads to instability of intonation.

The use of the other fingering, in which the first finger is placed on the two strings together and forms an axis around which the 4th, 3rd, and 2nd fingers can move freely, removes the awkwardness and difficulty of the passage:

The fifth as point of support and axis.

In an analogous part of the same movement of the Brahms Concerto, where the fifth is perfect, the awkward fingering of the previous example with the diminished fifth now becomes rational, for there is here no question of the first finger crossing from one string to the next, and the fifth naturally becomes the point of support and axis:

In the following passage from the last movement of the Mendelssohn Concerto there are hidden diminished fifths when using the normal fingering:

Allegro vivace   Mendelssohn, *Concerto*, 3rd Mvt.

Crossing the third finger over the strings in fast tempi presents considerable difficulties. A fingering using the position of the fifth both as a point of support and as an axis eliminates these difficulties.

Implied point of support and axis.

Let us take a few analogous examples from other works :

Bezekirsky recommends that one should not cross from one string to the next even when the fifth is perfect. ' If fifths are met with in a melody, I avoid putting the same finger on two strings ; this leads to uninteresting phrasing ':[1]

Later Bezekirsky gives the following examples :

[1] V. Bezekirsky, *A short historical survey of violin playing in the 17th and 18th centuries* (Kiev, 1913), p. 46.

CHAPTER V

POSITIONS

The term position is used to describe that position of the left hand, defined by the relation of thumb and first finger, from which it is possible to play a given succession of notes without moving the hand.

The location of the position is defined by the distance of the first finger from the nut. As this distance changes, and with it the position of the thumb, effected by successive movements of the hand along the neck in tones and semitones, so the finger-board is divided into positions.

The first position is that in which the first finger produces the interval of a major, minor, or sometimes even an augmented second, depending on the tonality. For example:

The division of the finger-board into positions is a convenient way of helping beginners to gain command of the finger-board. Numbering the positions makes it possible to specify the precise movements of the fingers along mentally predetermined divisions, and develops a feeling for the distances involved.

Such a numerical division is less necessary for the more advanced violinist. The concept of positions loses its significance, and can indeed be a bar to progress, as it limits freedom of orientating oneself on the finger-board. The actual position of the left hand during playing is often in contradiction to the generally accepted numerical position. This leads to an unnecessary confusion in the violinist's mind, and is the source of serious errors in the choice of fingering.

In modern playing practice various other ways of placing the fingers on the finger-board are widely used, such as enharmonic changes and the simultaneous use of two positions. In such cases it is impossible to determine exactly in what position the hand is. For example:

From this it is obvious that we must consider the position as a temporary point of departure for the activity of the fingers, which changes all the time to suit the specific requirements of the music being played.

The definition of position given at the beginning of the chapter implies that the number of positions must correspond to the number of semitones that can be produced on any one string. This concept is an advance on the generally accepted system of dividing the finger-board into tones and semitones, which limits the number of these points of departure.

That there is a certain lack of consistency in the present system becomes obvious in enharmonic changes. Thus an enharmonic change of one note or a series of notes, using the same fingering, is no reason for considering them as being in different positions. For example:

The generally accepted principle of positions would place the two examples given above in two different positions, as if demanding a change in the position of the hand which in fact does not occur.

Only a change of fingering in an enharmonically altered passage leads to a change in the hand position, or in other words a change of position:

Although the notes:

are approximately in the same place on the string, they are in the first position when taken by the second finger, and in the second position when taken by the first finger. The position of the hand in the first case is determined by the perfect fourth:

and in the second case by the fourth:

The extent of the position. The extent of a position on *one string* is determined by the distance between the first and fourth fingers, which form the extreme limits of the position. The most natural distance between the first and fourth fingers in the first three or four positions is a perfect fourth :

In these positions any interval in excess of a perfect fourth should be considered as an extension :

In the higher positions, as the distance on the fingerboard between intervals grows smaller, the first and fourth fingers can form the interval of a fifth or sixth while maintaining the normal disposition of the fingers. For example :

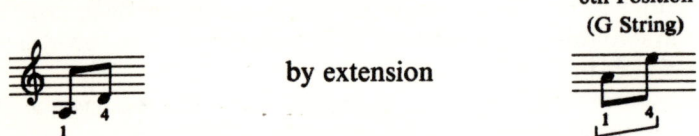

From this it follows that we must consider the most important part of left hand technique, from the point of view of establishing exact intonation in a given position, to be the positioning of the first and fourth fingers (in relation to the general position of the wrist, elbow, and thumb). This forms in the lower positions :

(a) the interval of a perfect fourth on one string :

(b) the interval of an octave on two adjacent strings :

(c) the interval of a perfect fifth on two adjacent strings, both taken by the first finger :

If we define the extent of a position by the normal distance between the first and fourth fingers, we should logically consider that the raising or lowering of a semitone by the first or fourth fingers, which alters the position of the hand in relation to the neck, constitutes a change of position. In practice, however, this is not normally the case.

If we consider the possible ways of placing the first and fourth fingers, which together establish the extent of a position, we find that they can be three. For example, in the first position:

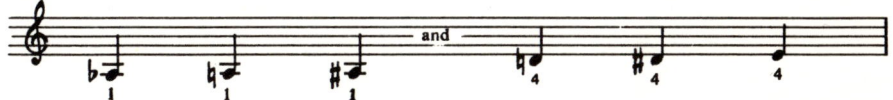

From this we see that the difference between the two extremes is a whole tone with each finger. If we consider the *normal* placing of the first and fourth fingers in the first position to be:

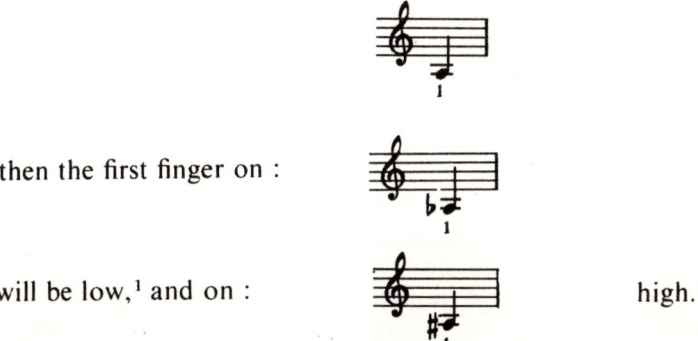

then the first finger on:

will be low,[1] and on: high.[2]

From this basis we can conclude that all the notes in the above examples belong to the first position, which gives an interval of a perfect fifth when both first and fourth fingers are extended:

The unchanged position of the hand

Extending a position to include a fifth or even a sixth is a device often used in contemporary practice. In the following passage from Ysaÿe, we have examples of a position being extended to a sixth and even to a seventh:

Ysaye, *Sonata No. 6*

Allegro giusto non troppo vivo

It must be understood, however, that this does not in any way detract from the significance of the fourth as the normal extent and intonational base of the technique of the left hand. Departures from this base are normally *transitory*, after which the fingers feel the need to return to their normal disposition. For example:

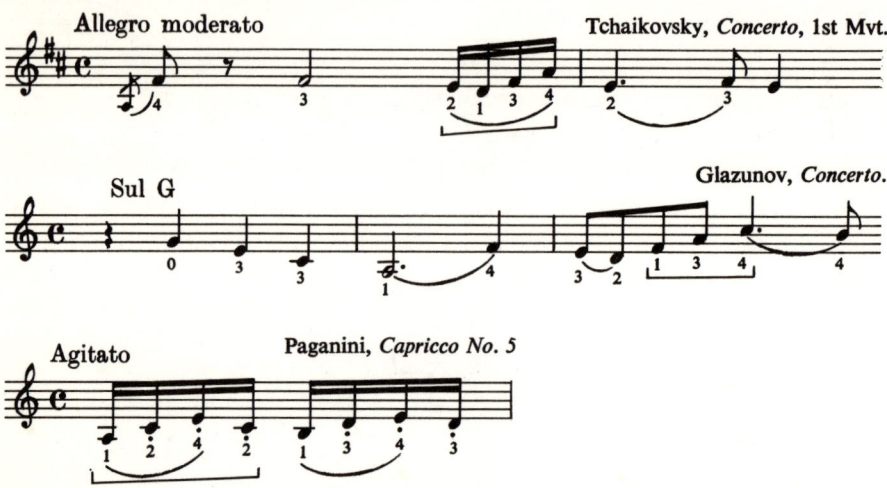

The rational use of positions opens up unlimited expressive possibilities for the violinist. The enormous artistic significance of positions in violin playing is based on two factors, peculiar to the nature of the instrument: (1) the possibility of playing the same note on different strings; (2) the possibility of combining notes of different pitch by sliding up and down the finger-board (portamento).

Owing to the fact that the same note can be taken in different positions on different strings, position playing is used to produce varied tone colours in expressive playing. The following table will clearly show the various positions in which the same note may be played:

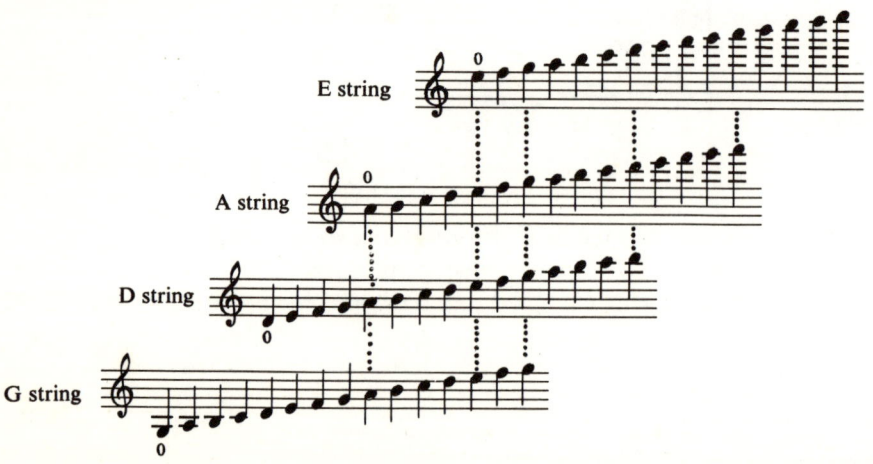

Thus the violinist can play the same musical passage in different positions and on different strings, using different fingerings. For example:

Tartini, '*Devil's Trill*' Sonata   Paganini/Kreisler, '*Witches*'

The extent to which the positions are used on the different strings varies. On the A, D, and G strings the lower and middle positions are used much more than the higher. It is only on the E string that all the positions are used. This is because:

(*a*) The use of the higher positions on the A and D strings and to a lesser extent on the G string leads to difficulties, particularly in fast passages (sounding adjacent strings).

(*b*) The tone of the upper register of these strings is rather dull. For this reason the higher positions on the A and D strings are generally used only in cantilena, where a particular tone quality is required (for example, in piano), rather than in technical passages which require a stronger and brighter tone quality.

The G string is an exception, and is often used throughout its compass. This can be explained by the particularly intense tone quality of this string, and also by the fact that playing on this outside string is not subject to the danger of sounding adjacent strings.

As we have seen, playing on the G string throughout its compass (sopra una corda) was first used by I. E. Khandoshkin, and was widely used as a virtuoso device by 19th-century violinists (Paganini, ' Variations on a theme from Rossini's opera *Moise* ', and many others).

Examples of the expressive use of the G string in violin literature are Wilhelmj's transcription of Bach's 'Air on the G string' and the introductory part of Ravel's *Tzigane*.

[1] The enharmonic change :

together with a corresponding movement of hand and thumb nearer to the nut than in first position, gives a position of the hand known as the half position.

[2] The terminology normal, low, and high was used by Joachim and Moser (op. cit., part I, p. 35). However, Joachim and Moser do not talk of different placings of a finger within a position, but rather of different positions of the left hand, according to its movements along the neck. This is contrary to the concept of positions given by the present author. In point of fact this leads Joachim and Moser to the division of the fingerboard into semitonal positions.

CHAPTER VI

CHANGES OF POSITION

Playing within the limits of a single position presents no real difficulty for the left hand. Auer makes this quite clear when he states that ' we should consider that left hand technique begins only with changes of position.'[1]

Smooth changes of position depend to a large extent not only on the skill of the violinist, but on the use of rational fingerings while changing. Bad and irrational fingerings react on the quality of the position change, making it more noticeable and uneven.

We must distinguish when choosing fingerings between : (a) position changes with intervals of a second, third, or fourth, and (b) position changes with intervals of a fifth, sixth, seventh, octave, tenth, etc.

The following aids to position changing exist :

(1) sliding with one finger.
(2) sliding with one finger, with the next finger then being placed above or below it.
(3) contractions.
(4) extensions.
(5) in certain cases it is also possible to effect a position change simply by moving the hand along the neck, without sliding, using the sound of the open string.

In practice, the most generally used method is the second. In this case, a correct position change consists in a light sliding along the string so as to bring the hand smoothly into its new position. The sliding of the finger should be unnoticeable, and for this the pressure of the finger on the string should become less as it nears the required position. Usually, the final point of slide is considered as an auxiliary note, the pitch of which is determined in accordance with the normal extent of the position as defined by the first and fourth fingers :[2]

For this method of position changing, we can use the following combinations of fingers : (1) adjacent fingers—1 and 2, 2 and 3, 3 and 4 ; (2) non-adjacent fingers—1 and 3, 2 and 4, 1 and 4.

Position changes can be effected by :

(*a*) adjacent fingers from lower to higher—from 1 to 2, from 2 to 3, from 3 to 4 :

(*b*) non-adjacent fingers from lower to higher—from 1 to 3, from 2 to 4, from 1 to 4 :

(*c*) adjacent fingers from higher to lower—from 2 to 1, from 3 to 2, from 4 to 3 :

(*d*) non-adjacent fingers from higher to lower—from 3 to 1, from 4 to 2, from 4 to 1 :

Let us examine the use of these fingerings in relation to intervals of a second and an octave from a given note on one string :

A comparison of the fingerings of examples a-f, with an interval of a second in examples a, b, and c and of an octave in examples d, e, and f, shows that changes in fingering produce different types of position changes requiring various degrees of movement of the finger which defines the new position. In example a from the 3rd to the 5th position ; in b from the 1st to the 5th ; in c from the 4th to the 2nd ; in d from the 4th to the 8th ; in e from the 2nd to the 8th ; in f from the 1st to the 11th.

The rational fingering in such examples is that which requires least movement of the left hand. In the first group this is that using adjacent fingers—example a.   In the second group it is that using non-adjacent fingers, lower to higher—example d.

This leads us to the conclusion that the most rational fingering for any position change over any interval is that which goes to the nearest possible position, in other words, as seen from the above examples, using adjacent fingers when moving an interval of a second, third or fourth, and using non-adjacent fingers, lower to higher, when moving a fifth, sixth, seventh, octave, or tenth.

Changes of position may also be effected without the help of sliding the finger, but by means of extensions and contractions.   For example, the following passage may be played not using the normal method :

but by extending the fourth finger (without sliding):

thus extending the range of the third position:

The following examples on the A string:

may be played in two different ways:

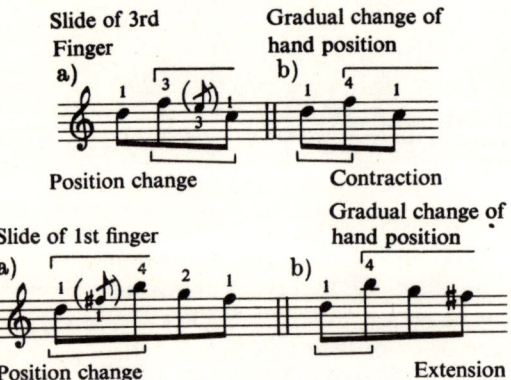

Thus a change of position may be effected by sliding the finger and moving the whole hand, or by contraction or extension without sliding, by a gradual change in hand position (a concealed or covered position change):

The use of contractions and extensions has a great advantage in fingering. It dispenses with the movement of the whole hand and reduces the number of position changes, which makes playing in fast tempi easier.

A change of position by means of contraction:

is made in the following way:

the first finger stays where it is while the fourth moves towards it, whereupon the first finger and hand make the position change. The normal form of concealed position change by means of contraction gives a whole-tone scale:

also chromatic progressions of the following type:

Changes of position by means of extensions:

are effected by extending the finger to the required position, moving the hand accordingly, and bringing up the remaining fingers. In choosing fingerings based on extensions, only the most rational forms should be used, taking into account that in the first three positions the amount of extension required is far greater than in the higher positions.

As has been stated previously, both extensions and contractions should be considered as *temporary* deviations from the normal disposition of the fingers, after which the fingers feel the need to return to their normal disposition on the strings (this applies to extensions).

In connection with all the examples given above, there are a number of rational fingering devices, facilitating smooth and unnoticeable position changes, which are not always sufficiently used in violin practice:

(1) Moving to an adjacent position by means of sliding one finger a semitone. This device secures a smooth and unnoticeable position change in *fast tempi*:

(2) Changes of position by means of alternating fingers on the same note.

Alternating fingers on the same note, particularly on the *strong beats* of the bar, underlines the rhythmic pattern, prevents so-called false accents, gives greater clarity to the sound, and also makes various tone colours possible on the one repeated note. This last possibility was utilized by certain violin virtuosi in their works, e.g. :

Wieniawski, *Concerto in D minor*, 3rd Mvt.

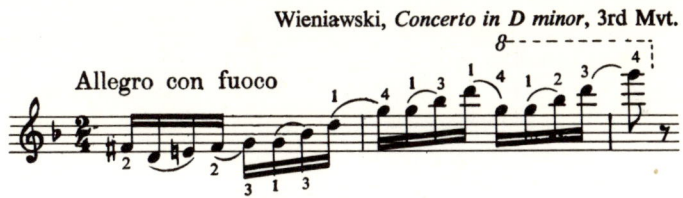

(3) Changes of position using open strings.

By using the open strings, the violinist is able both to change the position of the hand unnoticeably and to avoid the extraneous sounds which occur when changing positions in other ways. This device is particularly apt for changes to distant positions :

Paganini, '*Campanella*'

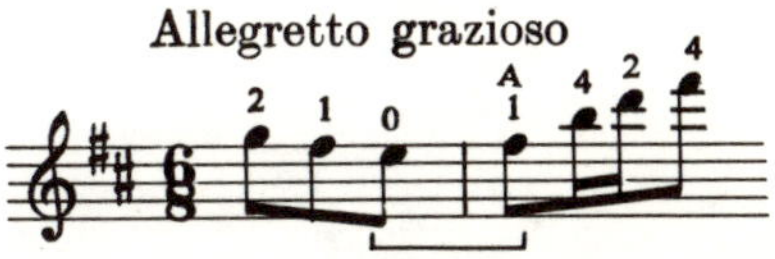

Beethoven, *Concerto*, 3rd Mvt.

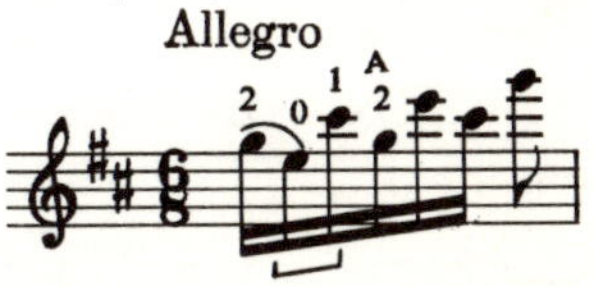

Brahms, *Concerto*, 3rd Movt.

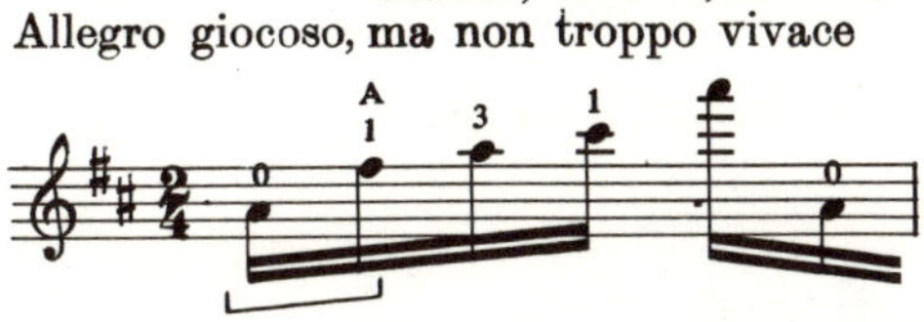

Wieniawski, *Concerto in D minor*, 3rd Mvt.

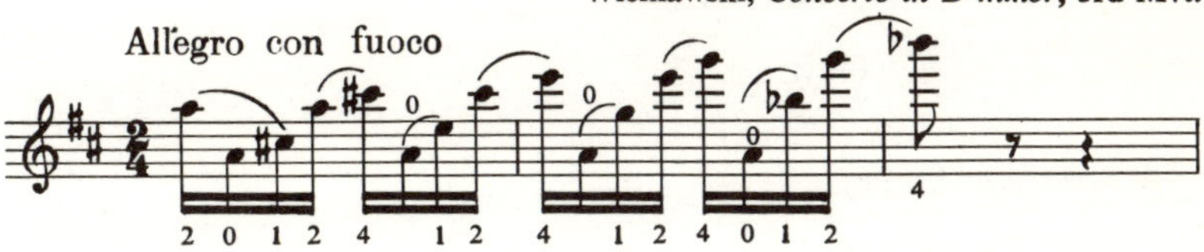

Beethoven, *Concerto*, 1st Mvt.

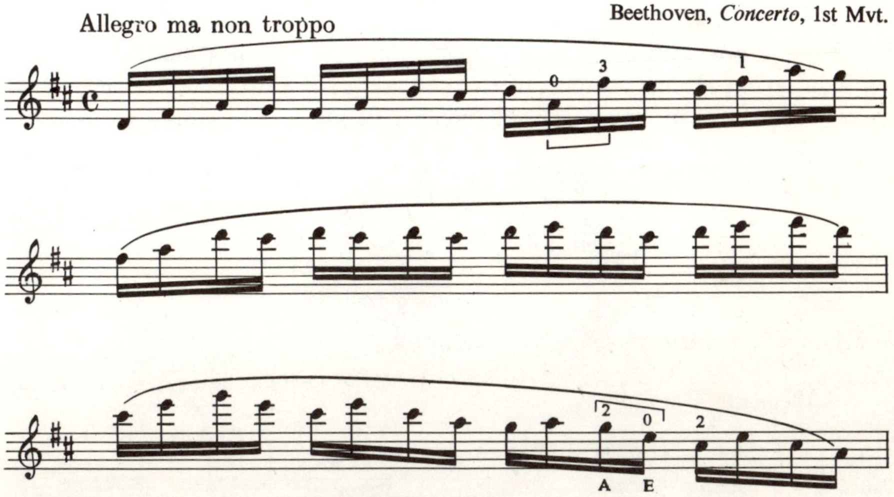

(4) Changes of position using natural harmonics.

This device is in many ways analogous to the preceding. It is well known that a natural harmonic continues to sound for a short while after the finger producing it ceases to touch the string. One is able to use this feature of natural harmonics to make unnoticeable position changes. The finger producing the natural harmonic, which is not firmly pressed on the string, frees the fingers and hand from tension at the time of moving to the new position, allowing the hand to move unnoticeably to the new position under cover of the harmonic which is still sounding :

For large jumps with one finger in fast tempi, the use of a natural harmonic often facilitates correct intonation when striking the lower note, allowing any necessary corrective movement of the finger to be made unnoticeably :

(5) Changes of position using contractions :

45

Allegretto poco agitato — Schubert, *'Bumble-Bee'*

(6) Changes of position using extensions:

Lalo, *'Symphonie espagnole'*, 5th Mvt.
Allegro

Brahms, *Concerto*, 1st Mvt.
Allegro non troppo — instead of

Khachaturian, *Concerto*, 1st Mvt. (ed. Mostras)
Allegro con fermezza

Saint-Saëns, *'Introduction and Rondo Capriccioso'*
Più allegro

Szymanowski, *Concerto* (Cadenza)

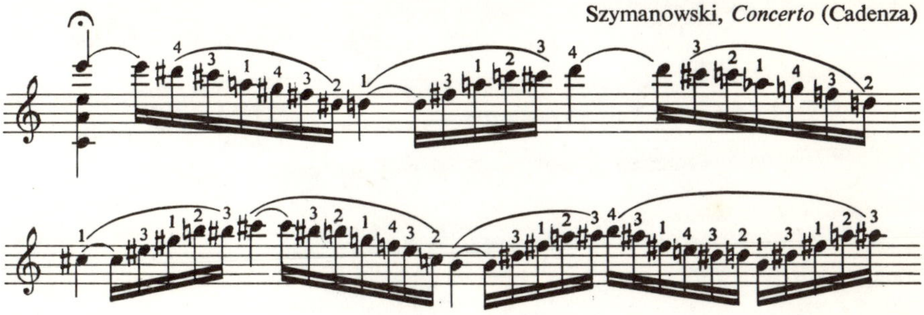

The same succession of notes can be played with fingerings requiring different dispositions of the fingers on the finger-board:

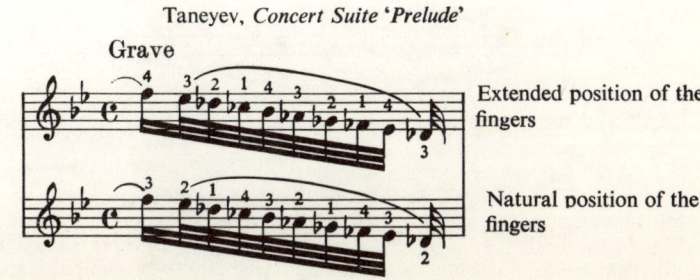

Taneyev, *Concert Suite 'Prelude'*
Grave

Extended position of the fingers

Natural position of the fingers

(7) Changes of position using a mixed fingering containing both extensions and contractions :

Fingering Chart of Position Changes on One String (by intervals of a second, third, fourth, fifth, sixth, and seventh)

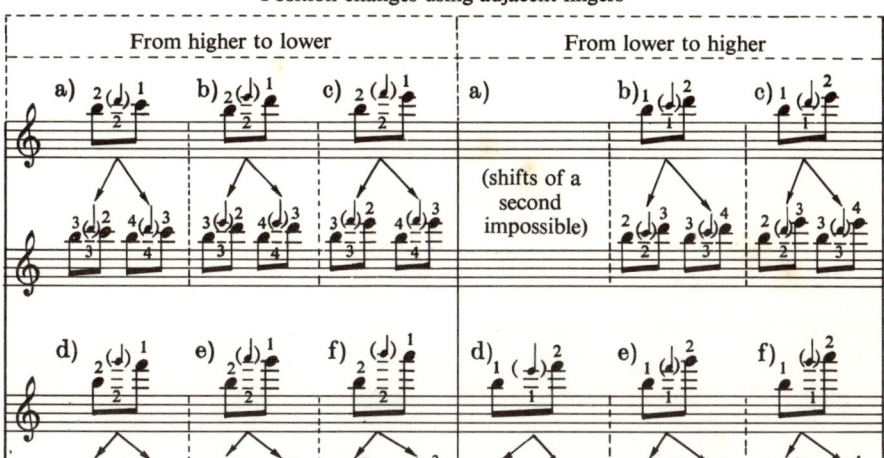

‡ Shift from 1st to 4th finger impossible
* Shift from the 2nd finger impossible

The same technique is used for descending intervals as for ascending, i.e. the finger already on the string forms an auxiliary note.

CHAPTER VII

THE EVEN-NUMBERED POSITIONS AND THE HALF POSITION

The use of the even-numbered positions (mainly the 2nd and 4th) and the half position has generally been avoided in violin playing, as they are considered less reliable as regards intonation than the odd-numbered positions (1st, 3rd, 5th, etc.). Bériot, for example, states : ' The odd-numbered positions are the most convenient for use, and it is not difficult to understand why : starting with the first position at the beginning of the finger-board the hand has a point of support for moving to the third position, thus securing correct intonation.'[1]

Even if this principle has some justification in the early stages of violin playing (although modern methods do not allow the palm of the hand to rest on the neck of the violin when moving to the third position) it is a grave mistake to extend it to general playing practice. The results of the avoidance of the even-numbered positions, stemming from these old-fashioned and incorrect ideas, are seen in modern violin practice in that ' the majority of even quite advanced players show a lack of familiarity with positions, particularly the even-numbered ones (2nd, 4th, and 6th). This can easily be confirmed by asking them to read at sight in those positions any passage well within their technical capabilities. One finds a feeling of helplessness and a sharp fall in tone quality ; one can't even speak of the quality of their intonation, it is so unsatisfactory.'[2]

Only a few writers of studies and other instructional material have realized the significance of the even-numbered positions. In the studies of Rode, Campagnoli, Sokolovsky, etc., there are occasional studies written specially in the 2nd and 4th positions. However, many fine players who have edited violin music (David, Alard, Auer, and many others) have systematically avoided the use of the even-numbered positions.

Such a policy leads to an impoverishment of fingering resources, and results in the violinist being faced with considerable unnecessary difficulties and awkwardness in playing. This is because it leads in many cases to unnecessary position changes, and makes the violinist use finger movements which are awkward in fast tempi, leading to uneven rhythm and unnecessary extraneous sounds.

Examples of this may be found in the following extracts from the Mendelssohn Concerto, the Lalo *Symphonie Espagnole* and the Vieuxtemps *Fantasia Appassionata* :

The use of the even-numbered positions in these cases considerably facilitates execution and produces a more even sound.

Even-numbered positions sometimes also allow one to avoid using the fourth finger. In a number of cases this leads to greater freedom in finger movement, making for clarity and stability in the execution of technical passages:

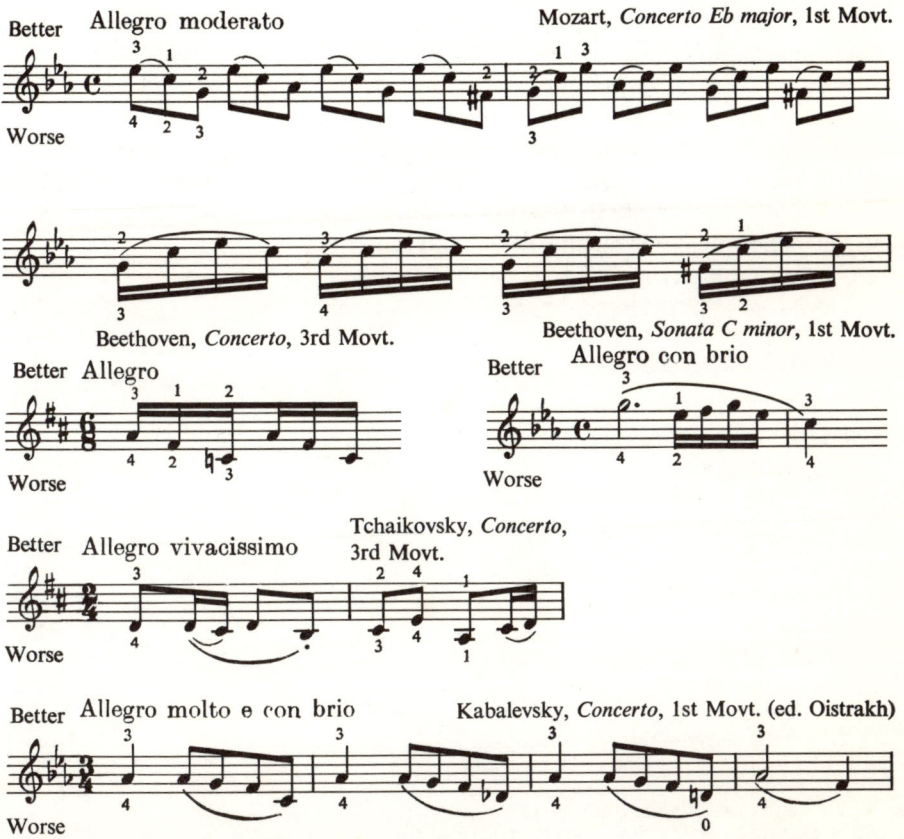

The use of the half position is no less important. It is connected with (a) contracted hand positions and (b) the maximum use of the fourth finger, which in this case is rational. The half position often does away with excessive and awkward finger movements and extraneous sounds, and generally has a number of important advantages. For example:

Even if lack of familiarity with the even-numbered positions and the half position were of no very great importance in the performance of classical works, although it would lead to difficulties and awkwardness in playing, it would certainly not be expedient in performing modern works, with their profusion of chromaticism and various kinds of augmented and diminished intervals, etc.

The extensive use of these positions should be part of every violinist's equipment, as one of the basic means of rational fingering.

[1] Ch. Bériot, op. cit., part II, p. 33.
[2] K. Mostras, *Intonation on the violin* (Moscow/Leningrad, 1948), p. 21.

CHAPTER VIII

DIATONIC SCALES

A diatonic scale on the violin consists of a series of tones and semitones using all the strings and in various positions, depending on the compass of the scale. The fingering of diatonic scales therefore consists of moving up and down the finger-board in major or minor seconds.

The question of how best to finger diatonic scales so as to secure evenness, fluency, and rhythmic flow has occupied teachers from the earliest times. This is natural, as the practice of diatonic scales is one of the most important factors in the development of the many aspects of left hand technique (fluency, pure intonation, rhythm, tone quality). The first violin methods of the 17th and 18th centuries already give fingerings for scale passages. In these, there are two clearly defined principles of fingering. One is based on the maximum economy of position changes, such changes, through two or more positions, being effected by non-adjacent fingers. The other is based on more frequent changes of a single position using adjacent fingers.

The majority of writers of violin methods of that period adhered to the first principle. In the method of Merk (1695) fingerings are given for scale passages in the first four positions, based on the principle of economy of movement achieved by moving directly from the first to the fourth position, leaving out the third and second:

Geminiani also adheres to the same principle. In scale passages he suggests that a position change should be made only when all the possibilities of the previous position have been completely exhausted. In the examples given in his *Method* (1739) he recommends moving directly from the third position to the sixth:

Tessarini gives the same type of fingering, but this time moving directly from the third position to the seventh:

Campagnoli, using the same principle, introduces a new fingering in which the change of position is made every octave on the key-note:

Leopold Mozart starts from the opposing principle, that of using adjacent fingers, stating that 'with ascending scale passages starting with the first finger, use the first and second fingers alternately'. For example:

Mozart also considers that a change of position on the strong beat of the bar gives greater clarity by concealing the position change, and he therefore relates his fingering to the rhythmic division of the passage. Thus in the following example he gives a fingering using adjacent fingers, but this time the second and third rather than the first and second:

In the violin schools of the 19th century and in the practice of the virtuosi of that time, we meet with the most varied forms of fingering for scales. For example:[1]

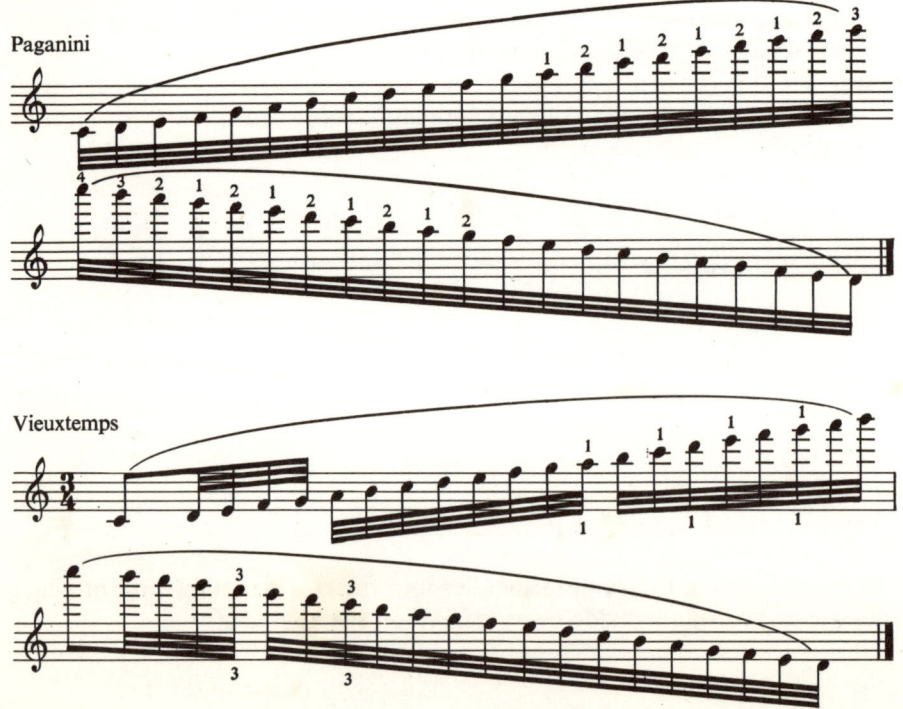

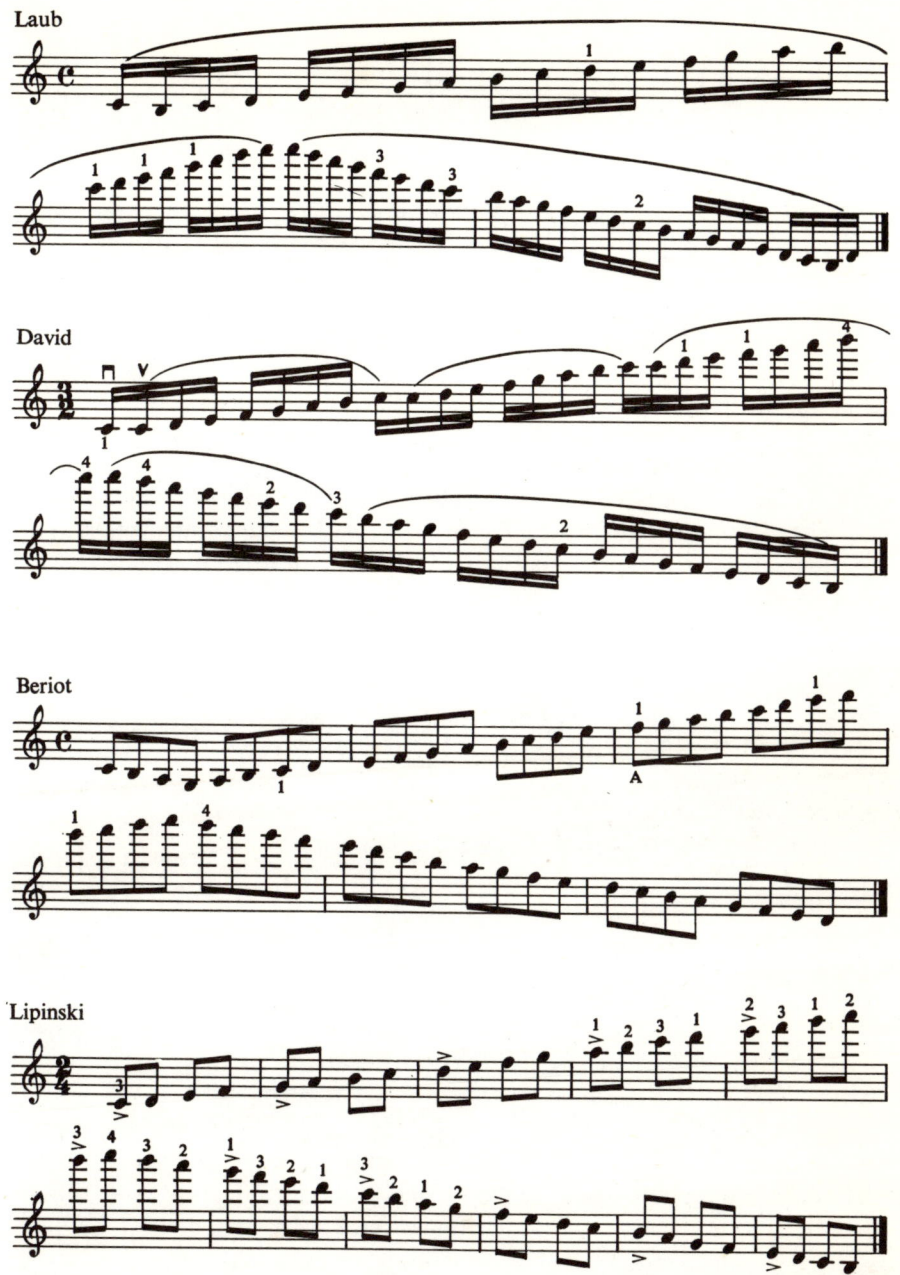

At the same time Joachim points out that the classical masters of violin playing, including Spohr, adhered to a definite principle systematizing the fingering of diatonic scales. For three-octave scales they started from the principle that each tonality has its own corresponding position. The root position of a four-note chord in any key determined the point of departure for scale passages in that key; thus for the scales of B flat major and minor and B major and minor it would be the first position, for C major and minor and C sharp major and minor the second position and so on, as is seen from the table given below. In other words, all scales (with the exception of those starting on G and A) had to be played starting with the second finger :[2]

The principle of playing all scales starting with the second finger depends on the equal use of the even-numbered and odd-numbered positions. It makes it possible to play all major and minor scales of the same key-note with the same fingering. Joachim, while noting the positive advantages of this fingering, pointed out that it is not always practical, as during the course of playing a particular piece, the hand may not always be in the position which should be the point of departure for scales in that key. At the same time, Joachim noted a number of other awkward features of this type of fingering.

Let us examine these awkward features, taking the scale of B major as an example :

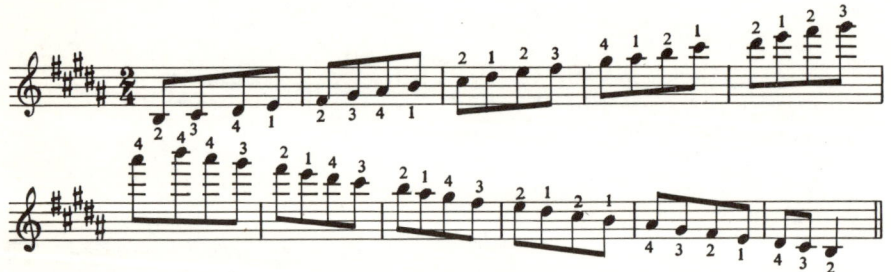

This contains the following awkward fingerings and difficulties :

which are normally felt when playing scales with this fingering, and which as a result lead to uncertainty of intonation (Ex. a, b, c, d, e) and bad tone quality (Ex. a, b) owing to the continued unnatural position of the fingers. The use of the fourth finger several times in succession (Ex. c) is particularly awkward in minor scales, when the downward step is a whole tone':

In such cases Joachim recommends the use of the following fingering :

In order to be prepared for all the eventualities which can occur during playing, Joachim considered it essential that concurrently with his scale study using the same fingering for each scale, the violinist should acquire facility in playing all scales starting from the first position. This gives him a variety of fingerings for each key, and at the same time helps to train him in the use of various fingering combinations.

A number of contemporary teachers have tried to lay down a general fingering for diatonic scales, starting from the most varied principles. Thus Wassmann, starting from the principle of the utmost economy of movement and the fact that the tuning of the violin in fifths gives a natural point of support for the action of the fingers in any given position, gives a fingering to cover all the scales starting with the first finger, which conforms to the fingering of Campagnoli given above :[3]

Jarosy, starting from his far-fetched idea of the 'natural' position of the fingers on the finger-board, in which the interval between the first and fourth fingers is a major third or diminished fifth, anything else being considered as extensions, which he categorically rejects, gives the following fingering which covers all the scales, but which is of little practical use :[4]

To determine a rational fingering for diatonic scales, one must take as one's starting point the natural position of the fingers, with a fourth between the first and fourth fingers. For the B major scale given above, this would be :

With this relationship between the first and fourth fingers, the fingering for all major and minor scales should start with the first finger :

This fingering, the result of the natural position of the fingers on the fingerboard, is based also on the principle 'each key has its own corresponding position' which was accepted by the classical masters of violin playing. It also does away with the awkward features and difficulties of the fingering for scales which starts with the second finger, and gives a more convenient position of the fingers on one and two strings :

Position of the fingers on one string

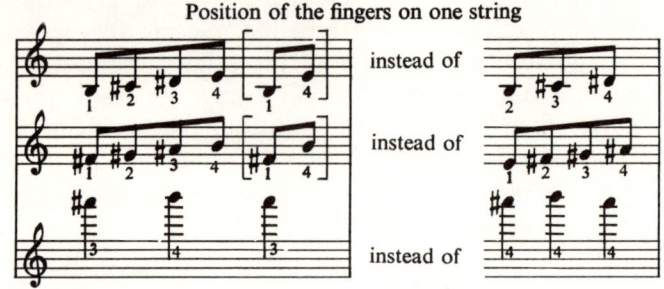

Position of the fingers on two strings

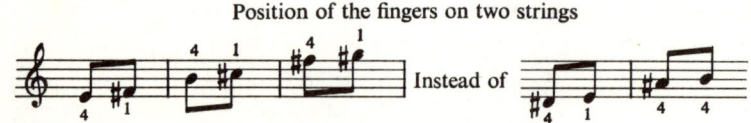

The fingering of scales starting with the first finger gives a better tone quality and greater accuracy of intonation.

Its superiority is particularly clearly shown by analysing the fingering recommended by Joachim for the scale of G sharp minor :

This fingering creates great difficulties of intonation. Joachim recommends starting the G sharp minor scale in the half-position, then moving to the first position. However, if one imagines the key of G sharp minor as enharmonically changed to A flat minor and takes into account that the fourth :

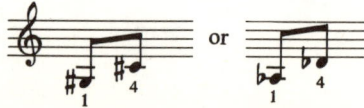

is in the half position, one does away with all the difficulties contained in Joachim's fingering :

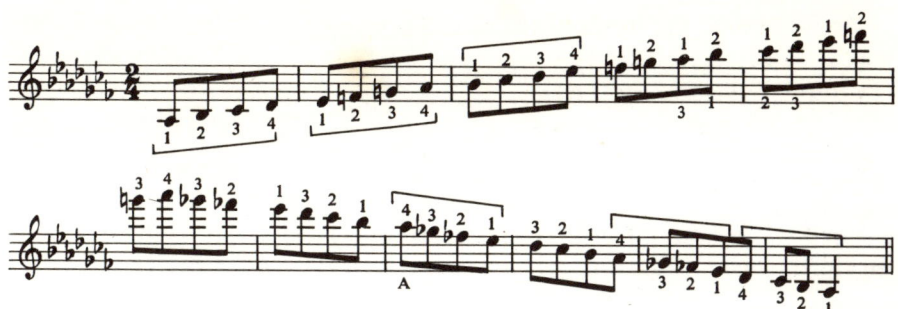

While accepting the general principle that the rational fingering for diatonic scales is that which starts with the first finger, we should nevertheless still continue the study of scales in all conceivable fingering combinations, for this undoubtedly leads to the development of independence of finger movement. I. T. Nazarov correctly sums up the position in his book *The basis of musical technique*:[3] ' Everyone knows that to play scales correctly (cleanly, evenly, and so on) means to play well in general. But in practice we often find this not to be the case; the student plays his scales well and his pieces badly. Here is a contradiction which in fact doesn't exist. What is wrong is the lack of understanding of the purpose of scale playing. The student who plays his scales more or less satisfactorily but his pieces badly has simply learnt those scales by heart with a particular fingering, as if they were studies. While in fact the purpose of scale playing is the following: the succession of notes we know as a scale is the simplest possible melody, which is easily and completely assimilated by the ear, so that it is easy to control purity of intonation when playing with different fingerings. In other words, the scale is the controller of intonation for finger exercises . . . The easiest way of acquiring complete independence of finger movement is by playing scales, and for this *one must be able to play them with any fingering.*'[5]

There are certain particular points to consider when choosing fingerings for scales. The fingering should be such that the leading note and tonic are on the same string, thus fulfilling the requirements of harmony that the leading note should lean towards the tonic, and ensuring that they have the same tone quality:

When intervals of a tone and a half are met with in scale passages, they should be played by missing out a finger, thus avoiding unnatural finger extensions which reflect on the purity of intonation:

In many cases of both ascending and descending scale passages, one can use the fingering suggested by Vieuxtemps and Lipinski, which consists of the repeated succession not of the first and second fingers, but of the first, second and third, which makes for economy of movement and clarity of sound:

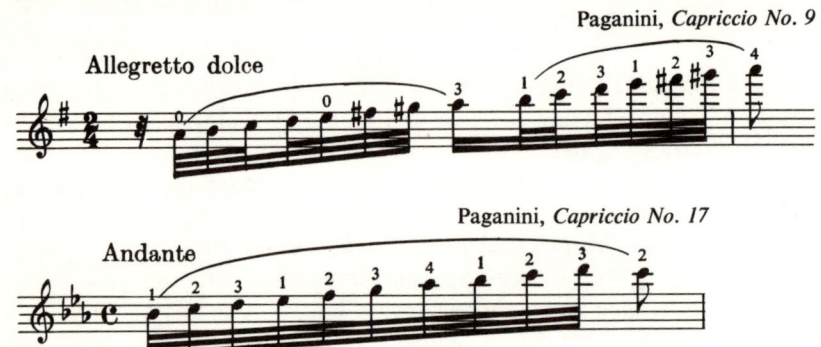

In choosing fingerings for scale passages, one should consider their rhythmic structure; the changes of position should coincide with the strong beats:

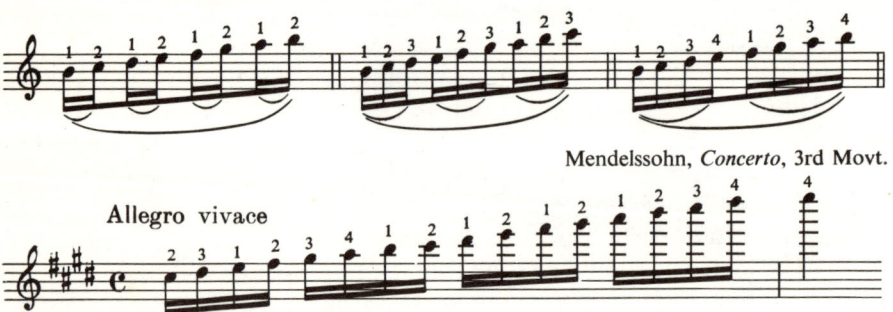

In scale passages one should not always adhere completely to the three and four-octave scale fingering:

[1] As given in F. Zhigardlovich, op. cit., p. 14.
[2] op. cit., Theil II, s. 167.
[3] op. cit., p. 19.
[4] op. cit., p. 40.
[5] op. cit., p. 10.

CHAPTER IX

CHROMATIC SCALES

The technique of playing chromatic scales and passages has been almost completely neglected in violin methods and books of instruction. In the classical collections of studies of Kreutzer, Rode, Gaviniès, Lvov, Dont, and others, there is a complete lack of special studies devoted to the development of this important branch of violin technique.

Neither do we find in violin concert literature pieces based entirely on chromatic scales and passages, giving such interesting and varied effects as are to be found in the piano concert repertoire (the famous chromatic study of Liszt and many other works). The only exceptions are the 17th Capriccio of Paganini, in which there are isolated patches of chromaticism, although this cannot be regarded as a special chromatic study, and the Concertos of Spohr, in which the technique of chromatic scales and passages is richly and yet subtly employed.

Nevertheless, the technique of playing chromatic scales and passages, which involves the use of various special fingering devices, is extremely difficult and requires special study.

In practice, there are three types of fingering which can be used for chromatic scales and passages, each of which is based on the almost exclusive use of one particular kind of finger movement : (1) in which each finger in turn slides a semitone ; (2) in which the fingers succeed one another in semitones ; (3) in which one finger is used throughout.

All these types of fingering, each producing different effects, can be used, depending on the artistic effect required.

(1) **Fingering in which each finger in turn slides a semitone** (the fingers extending or contracting while the hand position remains still). This is the most widely used type of fingering for chromatic scales in general. It excludes the use of the open strings, which corresponds to the rules laid down by the classical violin schools. Spohr, considering the question of fingering chromatic scales, writes : 'As the open strings (particularly the E and A strings) have a sharper tone quality than when stopped, they should be avoided when playing chromatic scales.'[1]

When playing chromatic scales, Spohr recommends that the higher positions should be approached not on the E string but on the G and A strings. As examples of fingering for chromatic scales, he gives the following two extracts from his 9th Concerto :

Spohr, *Concerto No. 9*, 1st Movt.

This type of fingering, requiring the constant extension or contraction of each finger, is technically awkward, and makes the clean performance of chromatic scales in fast tempi very difficult. It can be recommended only for the performance of chromatic scales at slow speeds. In such cases the use of this type of fingering does not present any technical difficulties and gives greater expressiveness of sound.

(2) **Fingering in which the fingers succeed one another in semitones.** The advantage of this type of fingering is that by doing away with the constant sliding of the fingers, it facilitates playing chromatic scales in fast tempi and thus leads to greater evenness of sound.

This type of fingering was first suggested by Geminiani and later developed by Bériot :[2]

It is the most practical and convenient fingering for chromatic scales. Its use over several octaves makes possible : (a) the use of the open strings, avoided in the old methods ; (b) the avoidance of the excessive use of sliding the third finger—what Joachim called one of the principal evils of violin technique.

In the example given below, we suggest making the position change on all strings after the second finger, and not the third as Bériot gives, which limits the extension of the position to a semitone :

Sliding the third finger a semitone is allowable in those cases where it is essential to avoid playing the final note of the passage on an open string, which is undesirable, as the leading note and tonic should be played on the same string in the interest of uniformity of tone quality. Therefore, chromatic passages which end thus :

are better played on one string, with the preceding note played thus :

We should again point out, however, that when playing chromatic scales in slow tempi the present type of fingering produces a somewhat *dry* effect. In such cases the fingering in which each finger in turn slides a semi-tone makes for a *more expressive* sound, as mentioned above.

(3) **Fingering in which one finger is used throughout.** This type of fingering is often used in fast chromatic passages. It should not be confused with the glissando, in which the precise definition of the semitones is not required.

Sliding with one finger is used : (a) on one string ; (b) most often for descending chromatic passages ; (c) preferably with the third, more rarely with the fourth finger. The use of the third finger is more convenient as it gives greater support to the hand while moving along the neck.

The performance of chromatic scales by sliding with one finger combined with the effect of harmonics is one of the most expressive virtuoso devices in violin playing :

Wieniawski, *Concerto in D minor*, 1st Movt.

Examples of chromatic scale passages:

Allegro moderato — Mozart, *Concerto in Eb major*, 1st Movt.

Molto moderato — Vitali, *Chaconne*

Allegro non troppo — Lalo, '*Symphonie Espagnole*', 1st Movt.

Andante — Paganini, *Capriccio No. 17*

[1] op. cit., p. 84.
[2] op. cit., part II, pp. 92–93.

CHAPTER X
BROKEN THIRDS

A succession of broken thirds in sequence may be played on either one or two strings with the following fingerings :

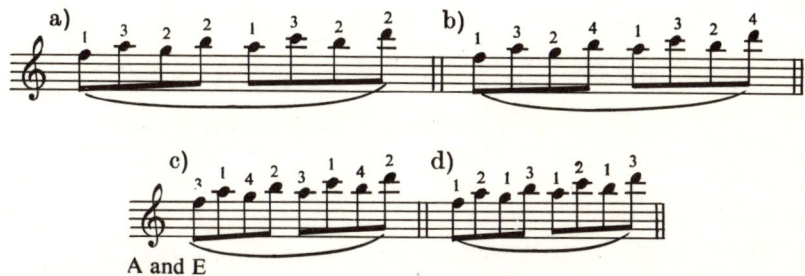

A and E

In each case the choice of fingering should be determined by the rhythmical pattern of the passage. If the higher note of the third falls on the off-beat, as in the following rhythmic pattern :

then the normal fingering would be :

In this case, however, the shifts to the third and fifth positions create accents in the wrong places, and a more appropriate fingering would be :

If, however, the higher note falls on the strong beat in a similar rhythmic pattern :

it is better to use the fingering :

rather than:

The next type of broken third presents no difficulty in the choice of fingering:

In triplet figures, to avoid accents on unstressed parts of the beat, the following fingering:

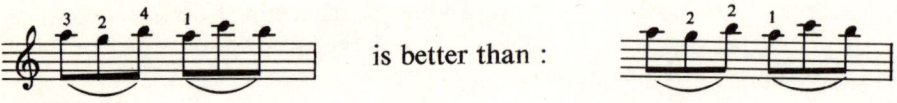

It is also possible to use fingerings for broken thirds based on finger extensions, both upwards and downwards:

Examples of broken thirds:

CHAPTER XI

ARPEGGIOS

It is easy to select the most rational fingering for arpeggios, i.e. that most common to all octaves, owing to the sequence of fifths and octaves in the various positions :

From this it would appear that one could conclude that the most rational fingering for the arpeggio is that in which the first finger falls on the tonic. This fingering, however, does not always sound well, and is justified most often in triplet figures. In practice, therefore, one has to use the most varied fingerings for arpeggios, being guided primarily by the tone quality required and the rhythmic pattern of the passage :

The varied fingerings given above can be used to embrace arpeggios in nearly all the major and minor keys, and avoid the unnecessary difficulties such as we meet in the following instructive examples :

Certain passages based on the minor arpeggio should be played not with the normal fingering 1-3-4, but with the major third taken by the 1st and 2nd fingers :

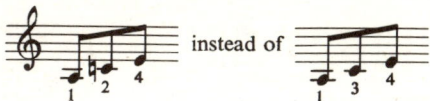

This makes it possible to avoid the uncomfortable strain between the third and fourth fingers, being more easily managed by the first and second fingers :

The augmented triad. The generally accepted fingering for the augmented triad involves (a) the extended position of the fingers on the finger-board ; (b) using the same finger on two adjacent strings, crossing over at an interval of an augmented fifth or a diminished fourth, which makes it difficult to secure purity of intonation :

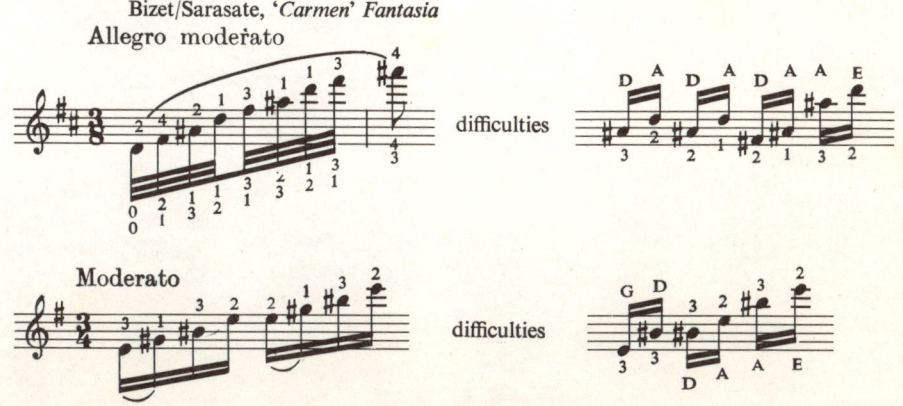

These difficulties disappear if we substitute a contracted hand position for an extended one :

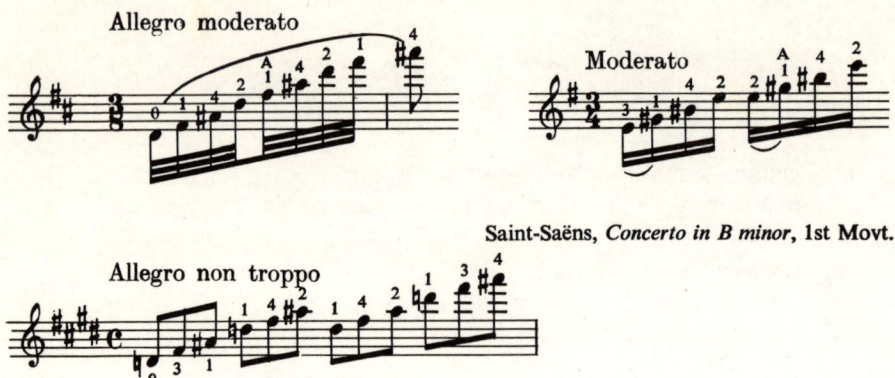

Saint-Saëns, *Concerto in B minor*, 1st Movt.

CHAPTER XII
SEVENTHS

A triad with a note added a seventh from its root is called a seventh. There are various kinds of sevenths, depending on whether a major or minor seventh is added to a major, minor, diminished or augmented triad:

It is those sevenths which contain augmented and diminished fifths which present particular fingering difficulties:

Let us separate these sevenths into their component pairs of fifths:

From these examples, we can establish the following basic fingering for the diminished seventh:

which does away with the difficulty of playing the seventh with the fingering normally used. Thus Sevčik (in his Opus 1) gives the following fingering for the passage quoted above:

This is awkward on account of:
(1) The extensions:

(2) crossing the strings with one finger at the interval of a diminished fifth:

Examples of sevenths:

Dont, Etude No. 3, op. 37

a) Allegretto   b)

Francoeur/Kreisler, *'Siciliana and Rigaudon'*

a) Allegro

b)

c)

Paganini/Kreisler, *'Campanella'*

Allegretto grazioso

Mendelssohn, *Concerto*, 1st Movt.

Allegro, molto appassionato

Brahms, *Concerto*, 1st Mvt.

Allegro non troppo

CHAPTER XIII
THIRDS

Thirds can be played with the following dispositions of the fingers :
(1) Natural :

(2) Contracted :

(3) Extended (mainly for major thirds) :

(4) In a few cases one can play thirds using the open strings :

Scales in thirds can be played with several fingerings :
(1) Playing in the odd-numbered positions—1st, 3rd, 5th, etc.—which is the most commonly used method :

(2) Playing in the even-numbered positions—2nd, 4th, 6th, etc.

Fingering using the even-numbered positions has one important advantage. As there is less distance from position to position, it allows the hand to rest half-way between the two positions. This facilitates playing in fast tempi and ensures smooth and imperceptible position changes.

The use of the open strings in certain cases when changing position makes it possible to avoid unnecessary shifts, the fingering generally used being replaced by the following :

instead of

instead of

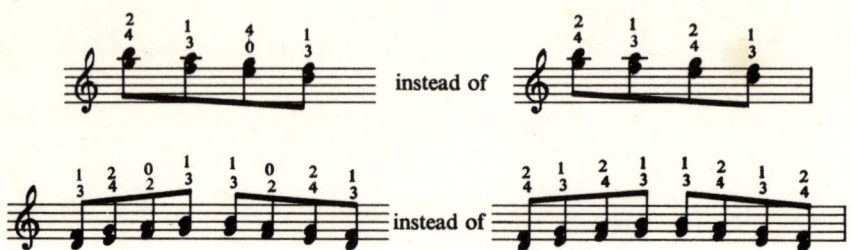

The choice between these various methods of fingering scales in thirds should be made with regard to the rhythmic pattern of the scale, which determines when position changes should be made. Thus :

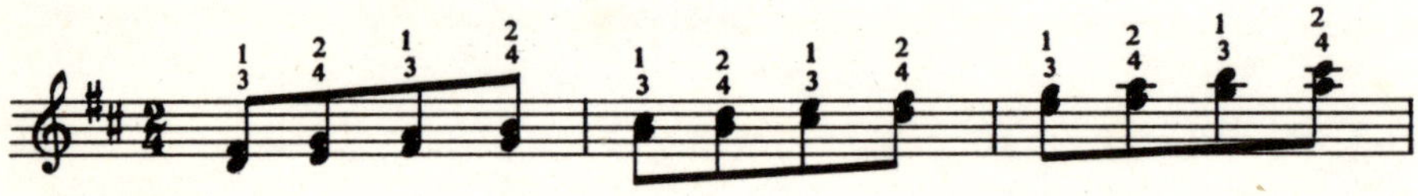

is better than

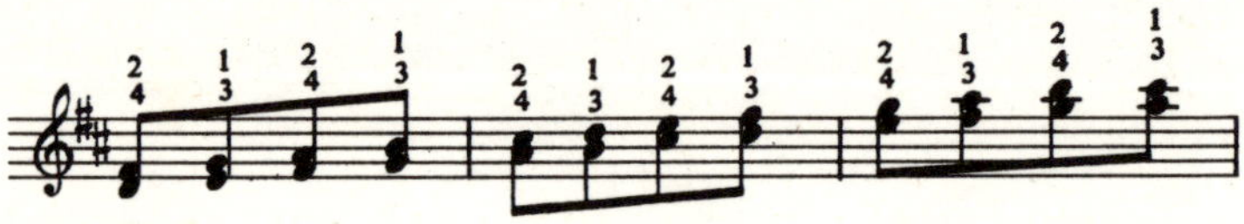

Maestoso

Paganini, *Capriccio No. 4*

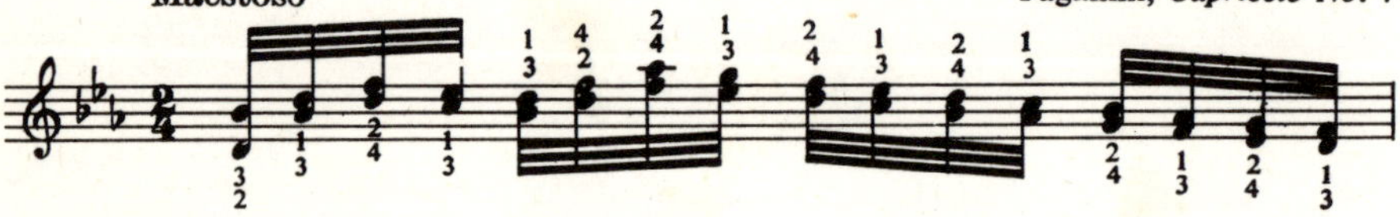

Examples of fingering for thirds:

Paganini, *Capriccio No. 1*

Andante

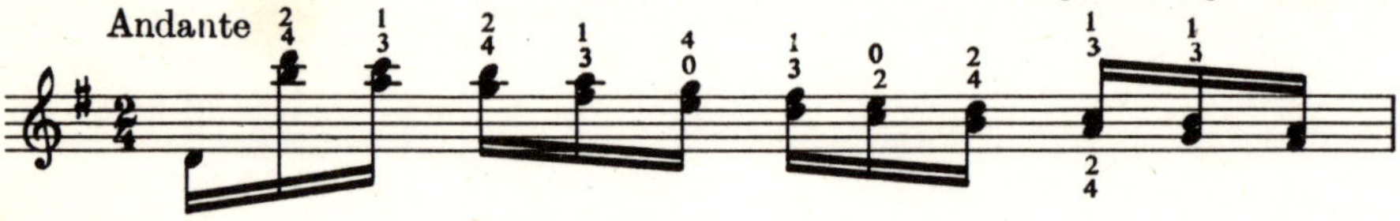

Paganini, *Capriccio No. 1*

Andante

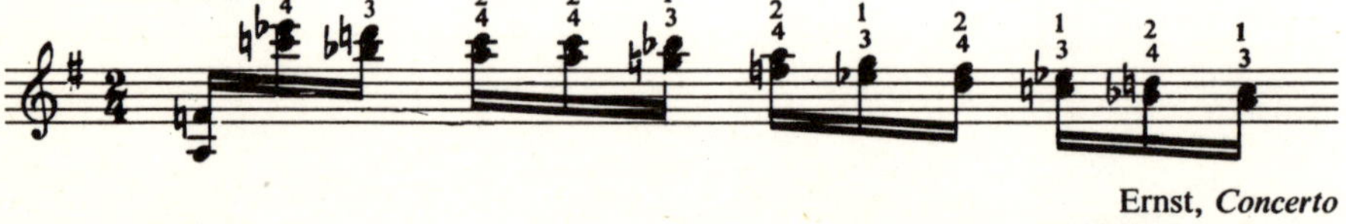

Ernst, *Concerto*

Allegro moderato

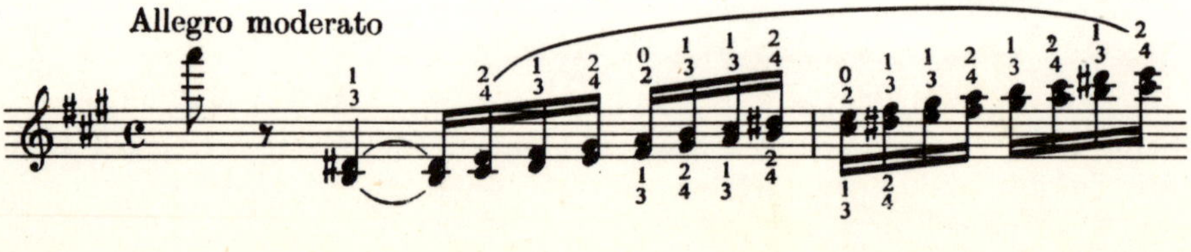

When moving from one position or one string to another, one should avoid using the same pair of fingers in succession, using the fingerings 1-3 and 2-4 alternately:

In the higher positions, the normal fingering is modified to avoid the fingers being uncomfortably close together, 1-2 being used instead of 1-3, and 2-3 or 3-4 instead of 2-4. This fingering gives greater accuracy of intonation and better quality of tone in the higher positions:

Chromatic scales in thirds can be played by alternating two pairs of fingers, or by sliding either pair by itself:

Paganini, *Capriccio No. 13*

The latter method is sometimes used to produce a special effect.

CHAPTER XIV
SIXTHS

Sixths can be played with the following dispositions of the fingers:
(1) Natural:

(2) Contracted (mainly for major sixths):

(3) In isolated cases the open strings may be used:

From this it will be seen that in practice the following fingerings are used:

There is no doubt that the following fingerings, which require the same finger to cross from one string to another at the interval of a diminished or augmented fifth, should be avoided:

It is better to use the following fingerings instead:

Fingering for scales in sixths :

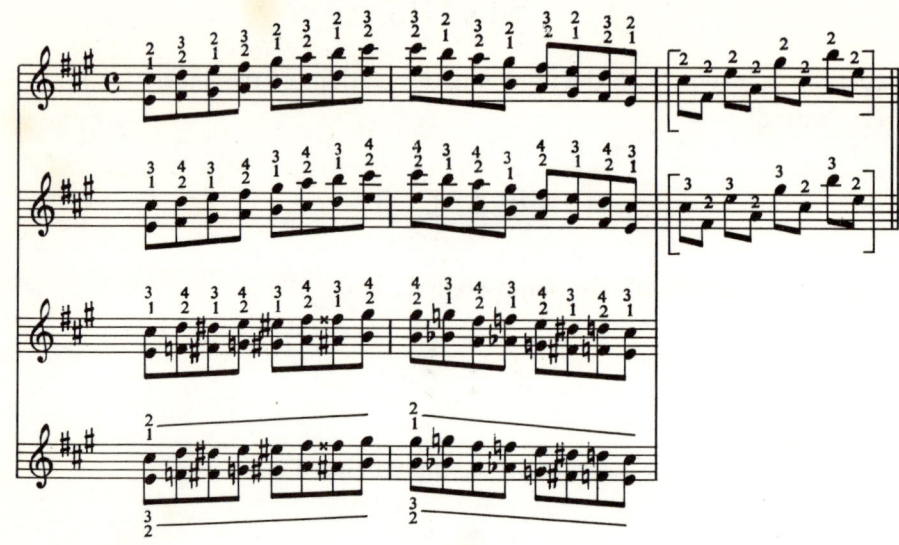

Examples of fingering for sixths :

CHAPTER XV

OCTAVES

Octaves can be played with the following dispositions of the fingers:
(1) Natural:

(2) Extended:

(3) In isolated cases the open strings may be used:

In practice, the following fingerings are used:

In the majority of technical passages octaves are met with in their so-called broken form, but in performance they are treated as hidden octaves:

In such cases: (a) in fast tempi the rational fingering is the alternation of the 1st and 3rd fingers with the 2nd and 4th, or of the 1st and 4th with the 1st and 3rd, which avoids unnecessary movement of the hand; (b) in passages requiring a cantabile style in moderate tempi, the rational fingering is 1st and 4th fingers, giving a greater number of position changes:

This type of octaves can be regarded in some cases as a form of hidden sevenths :

When moving in semitones in the higher positions, it is best to avoid the alternation of the 1st and 3rd fingers with the 2nd and 4th owing to difficulties of intonation :

It is better to use the following fingering in such cases :

Examples of fingering for octaves :

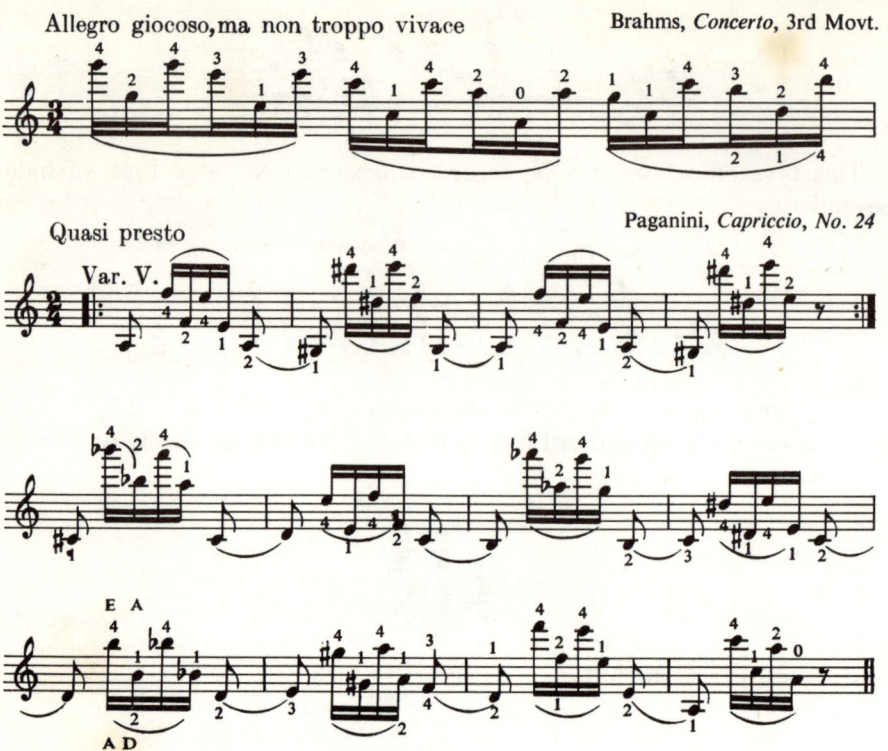

CHAPTER XVI

MIXED TYPES OF DOUBLE-STOPPING

The basis of left hand technique, whatever the fingering, consists in knowing how and when to leave the fingers on the string and to prepare and cross the fingers on the finger-board. In playing mixed types of double-stopping (particularly in legato playing) the observance of these principles is essential, otherwise there will be an element of roughness at every step, breaking the continuity. These principles are designed to give economy of movement, and are based on the fact that the nature of the violin makes it possible, when playing ascending passages on one string, to leave the fingers stopping the lower notes on the string without sounding :[1]

Thanks to this fact, all the notes are already prepared when playing descending passages, and it is only necessary to take off the fingers one after the other to produce the required notes.

The technique of pizzicato playing is also based on the principle of preparing the lower notes.

These principles may also be used for playing on more than one string, as, thanks to the curved form of the bridge and the use of the bow, it is possible to play on one string, having at the same time fingers placed on the other strings, thus preparing the required note which is then made to sound by means of the bow.

Leaving the fingers on the strings and thus preparing them, as well as keeping the fingers at all times as close as possible to the strings—these are the essential pre-requisites for mastering left-hand technique. Leading to economy of movement, these principles do away with unnecessary irrational movement. They are also *the final step towards the mastery of the technique of double-stopping*.

When playing on more than one string, these principles also do away with extraneous sounds when the bow moves from string to string. To them should be added *the preparation of the fifth* (holding two strings with one finger) which is in many cases a point of support for the fingers in a given position, making for economy of movement and stability of intonation.

It is essential, however, to underline that these methods should be introduced to the beginner extremely carefully and judiciously, as their excessive use can produce negative results, slowing down the free development of facility in finger technique. One must take into account that the free development of facility in finger technique for the beginner is in the first instance a matter of unnecessary and excessive finger movement (raising the fingers too high above the strings) and it is only by gradually eliminating these unnecessary movements that successful results may be obtained.

The tables given below should make these principles of leaving the fingers on the string and the preparation and crossing of the fingers on the finger-board quite clear, and demonstrate the close ties between these principles and the technique of double-stopping.

When different types of double-stopping are combined in a passage—sixths to thirds, thirds to fourths, fourths to sixths etc., the use of the same finger to cross from one string to another should be avoided. Such fingerings result from insufficient use of the position of the fifth as an axis, around which the other fingers can freely move, and make it difficult to secure a smooth and unnoticeable transition from one chord to another in legato playing :[2]

Finger preparations for mixed types of double-stopping :

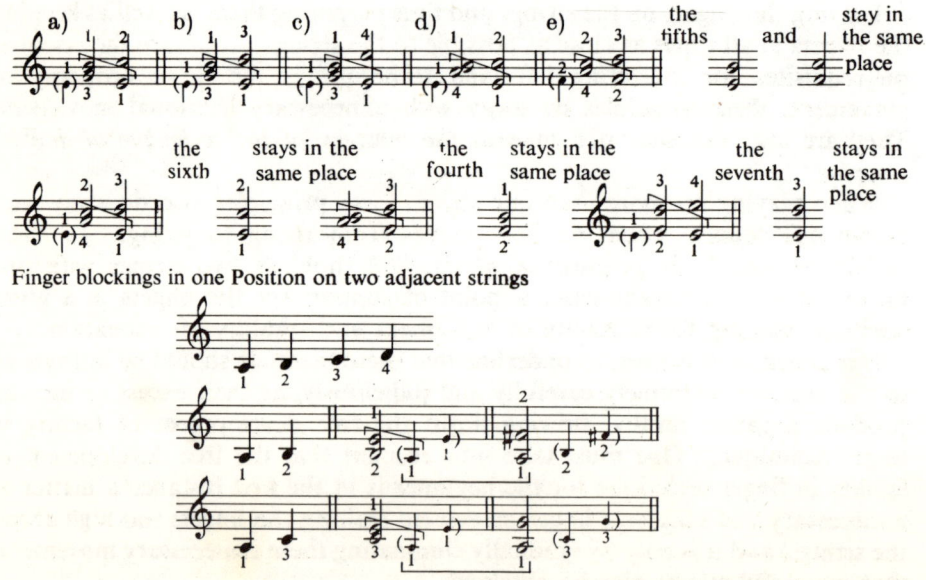

Finger blockings in one Position on two adjacent strings

The small notes in brackets show the finger blocking

Examples of fingering for mixed types of double-stopping:

Bach, *Sonata in G minor*, Siciliana

Bach, *Sonata in G minor*, Siciliana

Bach, *Sonata in A minor*, Fugue

Bach, *Partita in E major*, Loure

Bach, *Chaconne*

Brahms, *Concerto*, 1st Movt.

Allegro non troppo

[1] This principle is the converse of that which is the basis of piano technique. When playing the piano it is essential to lift the finger from the note as the next note is struck, otherwise, owing to the construction of the instrument, all the notes of the passage would continue to sound and cacophony would result.

[2] As seen from the above examples, the best fingering for mixed types of double-stopping is based on the use of contractions.

CHAPTER XVII
CHORDS

The technique of chord playing, even more than that of playing mixed types of double-stopping, revolves around the use of the principles of leaving the fingers on the string and of preparing and crossing the fingers on the fingerboard. From this point of view, chordal passages can be divided into two basic types:
  (1) Chord progressions:
    (*a*) with one, two or three notes in common in the given position:

    (*b*) with a fifth (where the fifth can be used as an axis):

Dont, *Etude No. 1 op. 35.*

When playing this type of chordal passage, the preparation and crossing of the fingers may be used.
  (2) Chord progressions:
    (*a*) with no common note in the given position:

    (*b*) parallel successions of notes:

When playing this type of chord progression the movement of the fingers and their crossing the strings are possible. If this type of chord progression embraces several positions then the following is possible:
  (*a*) Moving the hand and subsequently moving the fingers and crossing the strings
  (*b*) Moving the hand with the fingers remaining on the strings (parallel movement):

The following dispositions of the fingers can be used for chords:

(1) Natural: 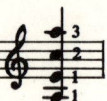   (2) Contracted: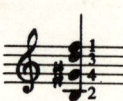

(3) Extended:    (4) With open strings:

Fingering for chords and tone quality. In three-part chords (with the third at the bottom and the sixth at the top):

it is best to avoid the use of the fourth finger:

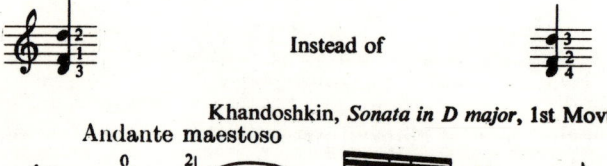

Khandoshkin, *Sonata in D major*, 1st Movt.

This **fingering** gives a better disposition of the fingers and **a better** tone quality. In other types of three and four-part chords (with a fifth) fingerings avoiding the use of the fourth finger also give better tone quality in the majority of cases:

Bach, *Partita in E major*, Prelude

Bach, *Chaconne*

Brahms, *Concerto*, 1st Movt.

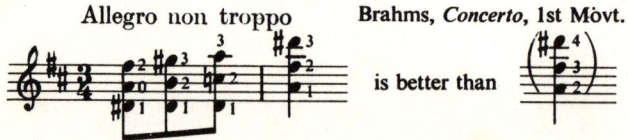

Leaps from one string to another should be avoided whenever possible, as they lead to roughness in the sound :

Use of contracted fingerings makes for a more correct and convenient mode of performance than ordinary fingerings for some chords :

In the 18th century, the thumb was sometimes used for chord playing. Thus in the Allegro from the 8th Sonata of Francoeur for violin and figured bass (1st Book, 1715) we meet the following fingering given by the composer :[1]

A little later, J.-M. Leclair gives a similar fingering for the following passage from one of his sonatas :²

A similar use of the thumb is met with in the works of K. Roieri, who in the preface to his 12th Sonata (London, 1740) explains that the figure 5 which appears in his 3rd Sonata indicates the use of the thumb on the G and D strings :³

Fingerings using the thumb did not become widespread in later performing practice, and were used extremely rarely. Occasionally it is still used today. Thus the Soviet violinist B. S. Fischman uses fingerings including the thumb in the following places in the fugues of the Bach A minor and C major Sonatas for violin solo :

¹ L. de la Laurencie, op. cit., t.I, p. 200.
² L. de la Laurencie, op. cit., t.I, p. 326.
³ A. Moser, *Geschichte des Violinspiels*, s. 181.

CHAPTER XVIII

FINGERING AND ITS RELATION TO BOWING

In many cases the movements of the left hand have to be subordinated to the movements of the right. For example:

It is therefore essential when choosing a fingering to take into account the technical difficulties which might present themselves to the right hand with such a fingering, and to try as far as possible to minimize such difficulties—unless of course one is aiming at a particular tone quality or technical or artistic effect. It must be added that such difficulties only normally present themselves in *fast tempi*.

(1) One should avoid fingerings which require the bow to cross over one or two strings:

(2) Frequent crossings from one string to another (pedal points on open strings are an exception) in short thematic figurations lead to unevenness of tone quality and are awkward for the right hand, creating difficulties of coordinating the movements of the fingers with the changes of bow:

(3) The suitability of a fingering is often decided by the type of bowing required by the passage, with which it should agree. A change of bowing in many cases implies a corresponding change of fingering. For example:

In dotted rhythms, using separate bows, for example:

the change of position should be made in the slight break before the semiquaver:

but with legato bowing, the opposite applies:

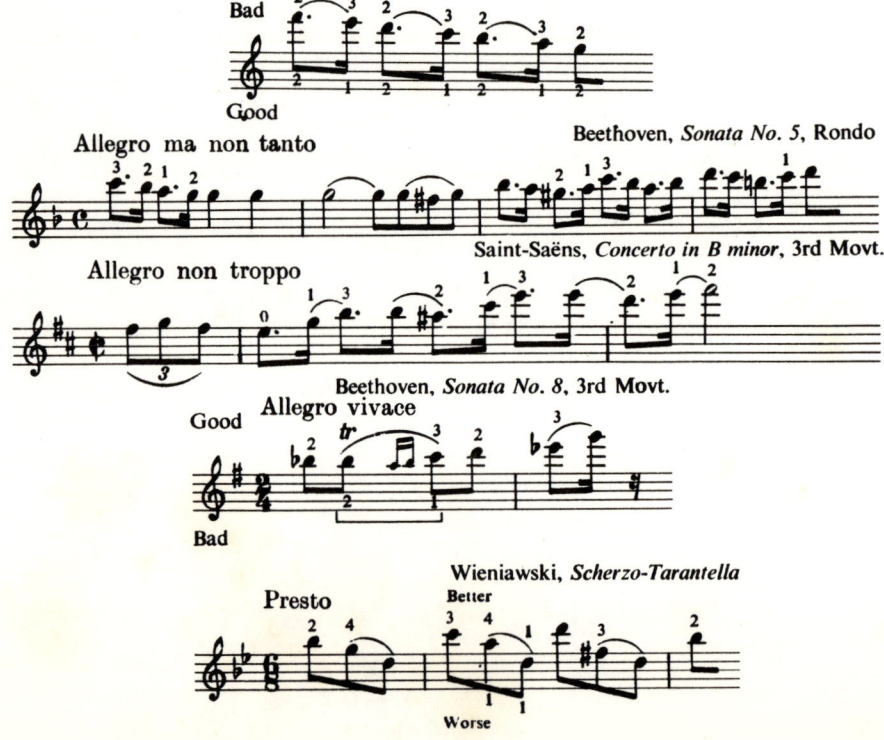

(4) In passages which contain hidden part-writing, two types of fingering on two or three strings are possible, according to the bowing used:

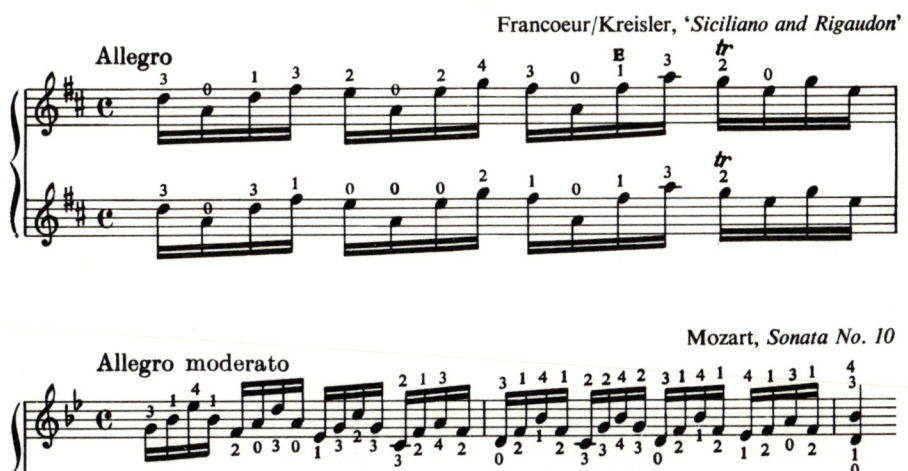

CHAPTER XIX

OPEN STRINGS

Open strings play an important part in the general tone quality of the violin, and in fact determine its characteristic timbre. As the different strings vary in the material from which they are made, their thickness and the prevalence of their overtones, each has its own characteristic timbre.[1] Thus the lower strings G and D are characterized by a thick and rather chesty sound, while the upper strings A and E are on the contrary characterized by a bright and open sound. Further, the different registers of the same string vary considerably in tone colour.

The judicious use of the open strings in choosing fingerings enriches the palette of colours available and intensifies the general tone quality. It is a scientific fact that those keys in which the open strings can be used have a particular colour, and sound brighter and more open. This is the result of the fact that the open string vibrates throughout its entire length, while the stopped string vibrates through a certain part only.

These special characteristics of the sound of the open strings have always been taken into account by composers writing for the violin. The vast majority of violin works are written in keys which allow the use of the open strings. It is not without interest to note in this connection that many violin works (three of the Concertos of Mozart, and those of Beethoven, Brahms, Tchaikovsky, and many others) are written in the key of D major. The overwhelming preponderance of this key can be explained by the fact that from it we naturally arrive at the keys of G major and A major for the second subject, development, etc.—keys in which the open strings can also be widely used (see the musical example on page 26).

Many features of the texture of works for unaccompanied violin are based on the artistic and many-sided use of the sound of the open strings. Among the most striking examples of this in modern violin writing, we may cite the Sonatas of Ysaye, Kreisler's cadenzas to the Concertos of Beethoven and Brahms and his own ' Recitative and Scherzo ', and other works.

Some special effects, such as ' bariolage ' are also based on the use of the sound of the open strings. ' Bariolage ' is based on the rapid alternation of two adjacent strings, one open and the other fingered, defining the melody :

In certain cases composers deliberately write works for the violin in keys which exclude the possibility of using the open strings in order to achieve a particular artistic effect. Thus Tchaikovsky's choice of the key of B flat minor with six flats, excluding the possibility of using the open strings, for his ' Sérénade Mélancolique ' was dictated by the musical content of this work, which demanded a more veiled and somewhat ' melancholy ' tone from the instrument. Works written in extreme keys, particularly the flat ones, are often met with in modern music. The fact that it is impossible to use the open strings in such cases makes the choice of fingering and the technical performance of these works considerably more difficult.

Despite the artistic significance, and in a number of cases the unquestionable technical advantages of using the open strings in violin playing, many writers have advised against their use. L. Mozart, for example, advised against the use of the open strings both for melodic passages and in double-stops, as he considered that their greater volume and sharpness destroyed the uniformity of tone quality.[2] Spohr, as has been mentioned above, recommended that the open strings should be avoided in the performance of chromatic scales.[3] Davydov suggests that they should be avoided in certain keys, in the interests of preserving purity of intonation.[4] Others reject the use of the open strings owing to a false conception of the supposed unexpressiveness of their sound : ' Who has not noticed that the strong and yet flat sound of the open string will cut through even a full chord, creating a bright but dead stain?'[5]

Considering the question of the use of the open strings from the point of view of rational fingering, it can be laid down with complete certainty that their use gives greater resonance, sharpness, and brightness to the tone, particularly in technical passages. On the contrary, lack of the use of the open strings dulls the sound. For example :

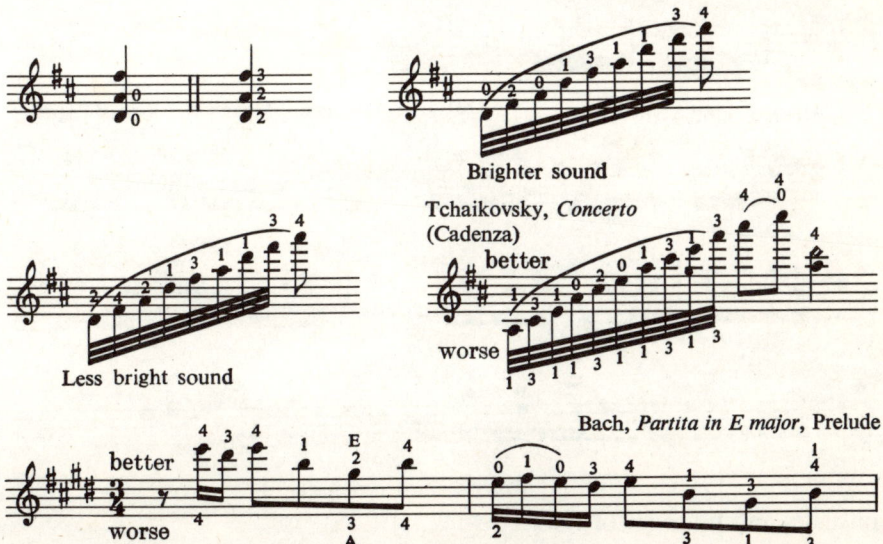

From the point of view of left hand technique, the advantage of using the open strings lies in the fact that it makes for economy in the movements of the hand and fingers. For example, in the following excerpt the use of the open strings does away with the use of the fourth finger, which to a large extent facilitates the performance of the passage and produces a brilliant effect:

In choosing fingerings one should make extensive use of the open strings, and should take into account the artistic and technical advantages of so doing. However, the performer should realize that in many cases when using the open strings with their bright and sharp sound (particularly the E string) he must take the necessary steps with both the right and the left hand to equalize the tone colour of the melodic fragment or passage so as to achieve uniformity. Thus in melodic phrases with a stopped note followed by an open string or vice versa, the extent and speed of the vibrato should be measured so as to make a gradual transition from the stopped note to the open string, and thus to equalize the strength and character of the sound.[6]

The so-called false accents which occur should be concealed by corresponding measures in the right hand. The following extracts from the E major Partita of Bach and the 'Prelude and Allegro in the style of Pugnani' of Kreisler are instructive in this connection:[7]

In scales and passages of the following type:

the use of the open strings should be related to the movements of the bowing arm, and the choice of fingering made dependent on the rhythmic pattern of the passage. For example:

The fingering which would give the best effect would be Ex. d, in which the point at which the bow changes strings corresponds to the rhythmic division (on the strong beat). Thus the correct fingering for this excerpt would be:

If we change the rhythmic pattern of the excerpt, then the best fingering will still be that in which the point at which the bow changes strings corresponds to the rhythmic division (on the strong beat):

Flesch gives the following examples:

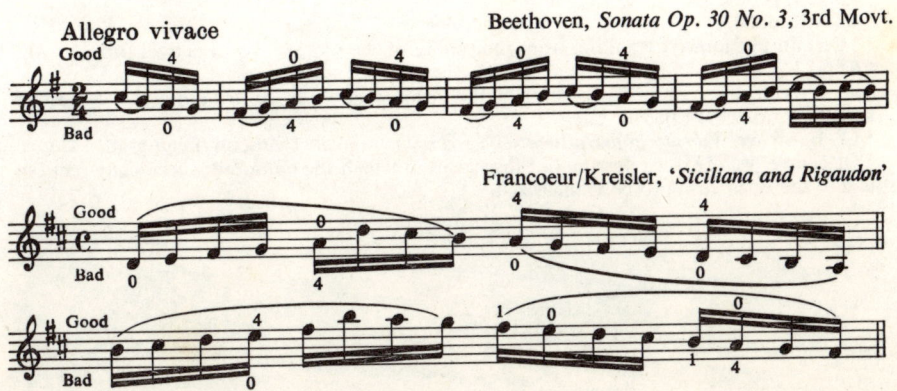

The use of the open strings as an important aid to imperceptible changes of position has already been mentioned (see the chapter 'Changes of Position').

The sound of the open strings also plays an important role in artistic phrasing, often serving as a means of strengthening the expressive contrast in a musical phrase. Thus the juxtaposition of stopped and open strings for a single note in a repeated melodic phrase throws it into relief and gives it a variety of tone colour:

An open string is often used to underline the beginning of a new theme or the division of a melodic phrase:

[1] Even strings of the same pitch, but made from different materials, have completely different tone qualities. It is sufficient to compare the sounds of silk, gut, and metal E strings.

[2] op. cit., p. 137.

[3] op. cit., p. 84.

[4] 'Certain phenomena resulting from the tuning of the violoncello in perfect fifths.' *Musical leaflet* (1873), No. 8.

[5] A. Avraamov. 'The open strings of the string section as contributing to false orchestral sound.' *Music* (1915), No. 222.

[6] Cf. B. Struve, *Vibrato in performance on string instruments* (Moscow/Leningrad, 1933), p. 41.

[7] Of course, we are not referring to those cases in which the composer specifically requests the sound of the open string to be emphasized.

CHAPTER XX

THE RECURRING FINGER PATTERN

In the so-called *technical passages* in violin compositions the choice of fingering should aim basically at brilliance, a singing quality of tone, and smoothness of execution. In analysing fingering methods one comes to the following conclusion: the most important device for simplifying the learning of these so-called technical passages is the use of the *recurring finger pattern*. By this I mean using the same fingers in succession over a number of different positions.

A good example of such simplification is the use of so-called rhythmic fingering in the following passage from the 17th Capriccio of Paganini:

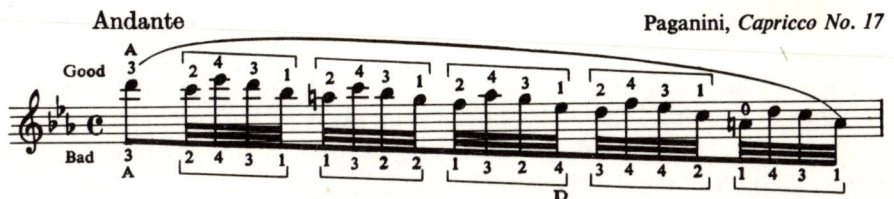

The rational fingering for the passage given above is the use of a recurring finger pattern—2, 4, 3, 1—as opposed to the unsatisfactory fingering using different combinations of fingers for each group—2, 4, 3, 1, then 1, 3, 2, 2; 1, 3, 2, 4; 3, 4, 4, 2; 1, 4, 3, 1, as is given in the edition of J. Becker.

Even more instructive as an example of the use of the recurring finger pattern is the following excerpt from the 'Prelude and Allegro in the style of Pugnani' of Kreisler:

The recurring finger pattern for this passage is the following: for the upward progression of semiquavers in the first four bars:

i.e. 3, 4, 2, 3, 1, 2 ; and for the downward (from the fifth bar) :

i.e. 1, 2, 3, 4, 2, 3.

The rational justification for the recurring finger pattern is that the only difficulty to overcome when using it is the exact movement of the hand to the next position, while maintaining a *uniform combination of finger movements in all positions*. This facilitates ' remembering ' the movement, and considerably simplifies the learning of technical passages.

The recurring finger pattern is largely based on making the changes of position agree with the rhythmic groupings, and in this respect it is in part identical with so-called rhythmic fingering, to which Auer attached such great importance : ' The pupil should be guided principally by " rhythmic fingering ", that is, he should make his changes of position as his rhythmic instinct dictates.'[1] ' Students and musicians,' further continues Auer, ' will do well to beware of the anti-rhythmical fingerings shown in the previous examples, the use of which destroys the sense and character of the musical phrase.'

The use of the principle of the recurring finger pattern is by no means always possible in its complete form. However, its partial use is often suitable. The recurring finger pattern in its ' pure ' form can be used :

(1) For descending or ascending sequential passages. For example :

(2) For the repetition of the same notes an octave higher or lower :

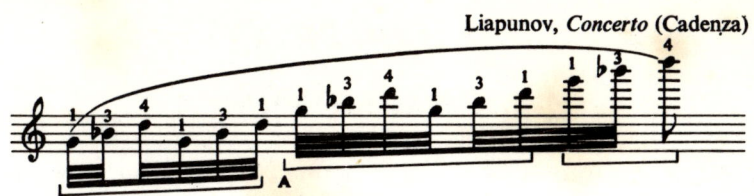

[1] L. Auer, op. cit., p. 85.

CHAPTER XXI

HARMONICS

One can produce notes of a special timbre on the violin, called harmonics,[1] and these are widely used in violin playing. There are two basic types of harmonics—the natural and the artificial.

Natural harmonics. A natural harmonic is that produced by lightly placing the finger on the vibrating string. Thus if we place the finger on the middle of the G string, dividing it into two equal parts, we can produce the second note of the harmonic series, an octave above the fundamental note (the octave harmonic G^1); if, however, we place the finger a third of the way along the string, thus dividing it into three equal parts, we can produce the third note of the harmonic series, a perfect fifth from the fundamental note (the fifth harmonic D^2) and so on.[2] In this way, dividing the string into smaller and smaller parts, we can produce natural harmonics on any segment of the string. However, as the natural harmonics formed by dividing the string into small parts 1/6, 1/7, 1/8, etc.) sound very weak, in practice one only uses those which a good enough tone quality to measure up to artistic requirements.

The sound of the natural harmonic may be compared in its delicacy to water-colours in painting. Their varied timbre—from the tenderly piping (on the upper strings E and A) to the thick and melancholy (on the lower strings G and D)—makes it possible to use these different tone colours as a means of artistic expressiveness.

One of the means of bringing to life the emotional content of a musical image, both in phrases of a discreetly lyrical character or, conversely, in perky dance melodies (in which the rhythmic brilliance has to be underlined) is by the use of natural harmonics on the upper strings E and A. As characteristic examples of this, we may cite the beginning of the Konyus Concerto and the passage from the mazurka ' Obertas ' of Wieniawski given below :

The distinctive tone colour of natural harmonics, particularly when combined with portamento, is used for the expressive underlining of a particular melodic turn of phrase which it throws into relief, thus giving a particular charm to the violinist's playing :

The expressive effects of natural harmonics can be exceptionally widely used, particularly in combination with portamenti and glissandi:

(*a*) At the beginning of a melodic phrase of a peaceful, contemplative character:

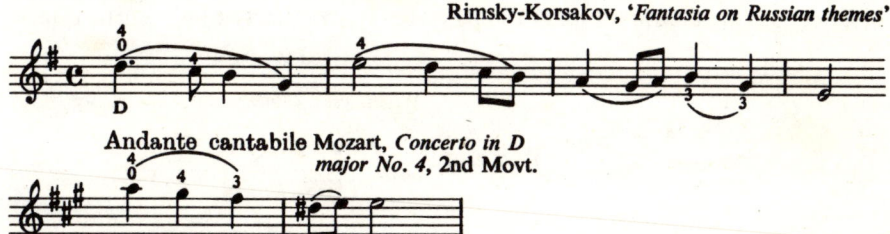

(*b*) At the end of a melodic phrase requiring a special limpid, melting tone colour:

(*c*) In melodic fragments of a light-hearted or graceful character:

(*d*) The replacement of the sound of a stopped string by a natural harmonic on the same note in *the repetition of a melodic fragment* makes an effective tonal contrast:

(*e*) The immediate contrasting juxtaposition of an open string with a natural harmonic, or of a natural harmonic with a stopped string, gives a particularly expressive effect. In the one case it increases the clarity and ringing quality of the tone:

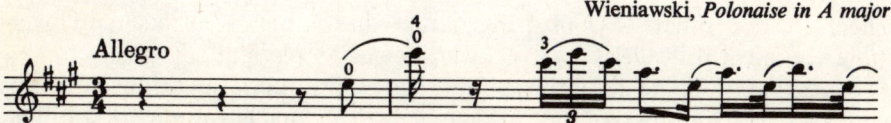

and in the other it gives a warm and gentle colour to the performance:

(*f*) The use of an accented natural harmonic at the beginning of a fast passage of a headstrong character gives the passage a particularly ringing tone quality:

(*g*) The use of a natural harmonic in combination with glissando at the end of a fast passage gives such a passage great virtuoso sweep and brilliance:

(*h*) In works with elements of scherzo-like fantasy, the use of natural harmonics strengthens the impression of 'flying':

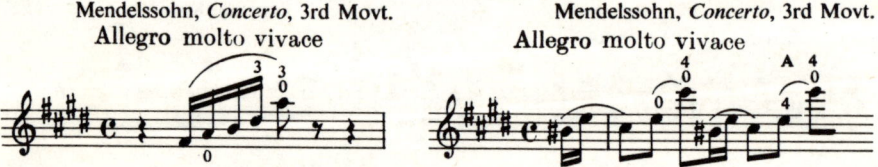

(*i*) The combination of natural harmonics and glissandi in short repeated motives gives an exceptionally brilliant effect:

The use of natural harmonics in many cases obviates or facilitates the technical side of violin playing. In the chapter 'Changes of Position' we considered the question of natural harmonics as an important aid to position changing.

There are also other ways of using natural harmonics as a means of overcoming technical difficulties and awkwardnesses in playing.

The fact that the same natural harmonic can be produced in various positions and on various strings makes it possible to substitute one harmonic for another, which often makes for economy of movement in the left hand and secures **greater** certainty of intonation:

In a few cases it is possible to use natural harmonics to avoid awkward string crossing with the bow:

Occasionally, in the interests of reducing the number of position changes, it is possible to replace certain high notes by natural harmonics. For example:

Table of natural harmonics (in common use)

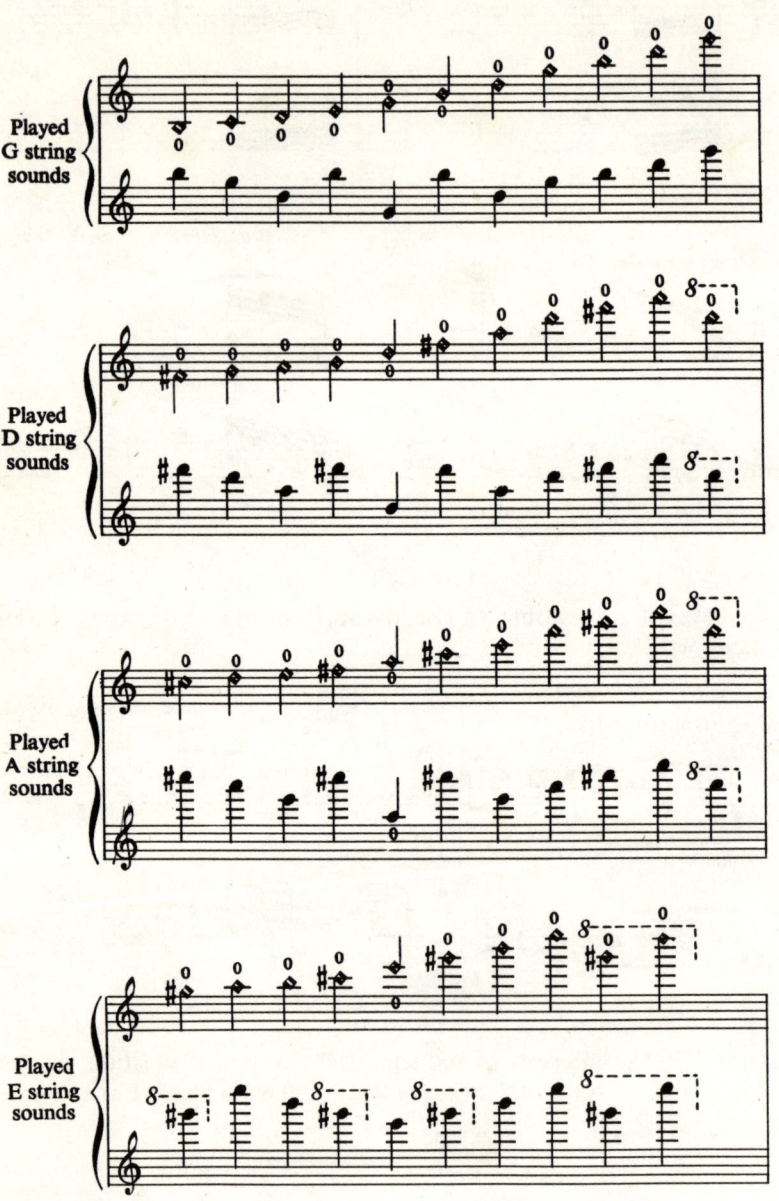

Artificial harmonics. An artificial harmonic is the sound produced by pressing (shortening) the string with the lower finger and simultaneously lightly touching the remaining vibrating part of the string with another finger. Depending on the interval defined by these two fingers, it is possible to produce various kinds of artificial harmonics (thirds, fourths, fifths, octaves). As the shortening of the string can be done chromatically, one should in theory be able to produce the whole chromatic scale in artificial harmonics. In practice, however, it is not always possible to produce the chromatic scale in artificial harmonics at a fifth or an octave, as purely technical reasons prevent this (the extensions

necessary are not always practicable, particularly in the lower positions).[3]
Below are given examples of the various kinds of artificial harmonics:

(a) At a major third:

These sound two octaves and a major third from the fundamental:

(b) At a minor third:

These sound two octaves and a perfect fifth from the fundamental:

(c) At a fourth:

These sound two octaves from the fundamental:

(d) At a fifth:

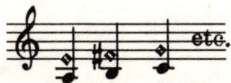

These sound one octave and a fifth from the fundamental:

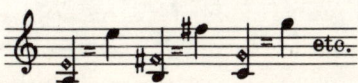

(*e*) At a major sixth :

These sound two octaves and a major third from the fundamental :

(*f*) At the octave :

These sound an octave from the fundamental :

In practice, the most commonly used artificial harmonics are those at a fourth, fifth, or major third, which produce a full and good tone. The timbre of artificial harmonics has its own particular character, which differs from that of natural harmonics in that it is possible to use vibrato for artificial harmonics. This gives a more emotional character to the sounds of the artificial harmonics.

Thanks to the fact that the same note can be produced on different parts of the string and in different ways, it is possible in certain cases to replace one type of harmonic with another, which can give economy of movement in the left hand, and avoids the necessity of making superfluous and risky jumps to distant positions :

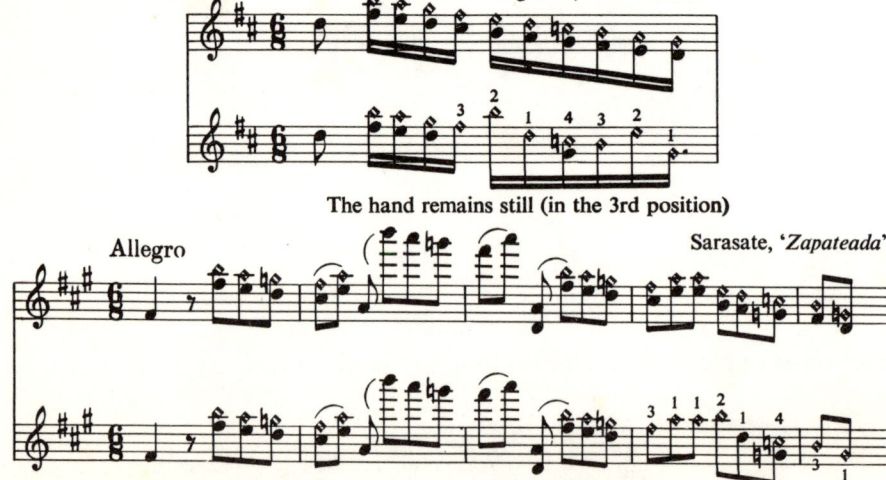

In some cases it is possible to replace successions of natural and artificial harmonics by the so-called false harmonics, discovered in 1928 by the Soviet violinist Y. B. Targonsky (as N. A. Garbuzov remarks, it would be more correct to call them secondary artificial harmonics).[4] For example, the following passage:

can be played:

This mode of execution does away with the continual crossing of strings with the bow, which is awkward in fast tempi and makes smooth execution difficult. In order to produce these so-called false harmonics, all the fingers, particularly the first, should remain on the strings. As Targonsky points out: ' In fast tempi and with a little practice, one can play by this method not only the major scales, but also any other successions of notes. Further, they can be produced with greater pressure on the strings than is normal with harmonics. For such successions of notes the fundamentals are not needed at all. In fast tempi, starting with the natural harmonic at a fourth, one can play the following passage on one string:

And, as was shown above, it is possible to change strings when playing false harmonics (see the ' false ' scale in the Etude of Ernst) which widens the scope and importance of their use even more.'[5]

In certain cases it is possible to use artificial harmonics to replace very high notes of poor tone quality:

By using artificial harmonics one can considerably enlarge the compass of each string:

Table of Alternative Harmonics

The formation of double harmonics can be worked out from this table.

Double harmonics are produced by the simultaneous sounding on adjacent strings of two natural or artificial harmonics, and also by combining natural and artificial harmonics.[6] Double harmonics are one of the most difficult branches of violin technique. The knowledge of how to replace one type of harmonic by another helps considerably to facilitate their execution.

Artificial double harmonics are found only in successions of thirds (major and minor) and perfect fifths. The technique of producing artificial double harmonics in successions of perfect fifths and minor thirds is comparatively easy, as in both cases the fundamental note is taken on two strings with the first finger:

Major thirds are much more difficult, as the fundamental notes of the two harmonics are at the interval of an augmented fifth, which has to be taken by two fingers, requiring an awkward position of the hand and fingers:

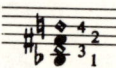

In such a case, using a natural harmonic in the place of one of the artificial harmonics gives a much more convenient fingering, which considerably simplifies its performance:

In the present chapter we have by no means exhausted all the possible uses of natural and artificial harmonics as a fingering device in violin playing. However, it will already be seen to what extent the use of harmonics enriches the violin's palette of colours, greatly enlarges the expressive resources of the instrument, and in many cases serves also as an important means of simplifying difficulties of execution.

---

[1] The first to use harmonics was the French violinist J. J. Cassanea de Mondonville in his Sonatas for Violin and Bass, published about 1738. He called them 'Les sons harmoniques'. (Cf. Laurencie, L. de la, op. cit., t.I, pp. 419, 423.)

[2] As given by N. A. Garbuzov. See his introduction to Y. Targonsky's *The Harmonics of String Instruments* (Moscow, 1936), p. 3.

[3] As given by N. A. Garbuzov, op. cit., p. 5.

[4] Cf. his introduction to the work of Targonsky, op. cit., p. 5.

[5] Y. Targonsky, op. cit., pp. 24–25.

[6] Paganini was the first to use double harmonics in his works. However, he gave no details as to their execution, merely labelling them 'Armonici'. As Targonsky rightly points out, this has made the performing of Paganini's works very much more difficult, as the violinist has to spend a lot of time in deciphering the double harmonics.

CHAPTER XXII

ENHARMONIC CHANGES

The enharmonic change is an important device in violin playing, facilitating the choice of a rational fingering in a number of cases. By simplifying the notation, it sometimes simplifies the perception of the relationships between intervals, and thus gives the performer a clearer and more exact idea of their position on the strings.

For example, the violinist will frequently play the following succession of notes with a fingering which requires an unnatural position of the fingers and which creates difficulties of intonation :

Whereas if the given passage were written in an enharmonically changed form, it would never have entered anybody's head to play it with such a fingering :

The advantage of choosing a fingering which gives a more natural position of the fingers and is thus more secure for intonation on the basis of enharmonically changing the notes of the passage is seen from the following examples:

The notation of the following passages from the Concertos of Liapounov and Arensky is even more complicated for visual comprehension, and prevents the violinist from quickly choosing the right fingering. By enharmonically changing the passage, thus simplifying the notation, it becomes much clearer and enables the violinist to make the right choice :

The violinist who has not developed the habit of choosing his fingering on the basis of mentally making an enharmonic change, may at first find a certain difficulty in so doing. But this is only psychological and can be overcome by a certain amount of practice to develop the necessary knack.

CHAPTER XXIII

FINGERING AND INTONATION

The purity of the violinist's intonation depends to a certain extent on his choice of fingering. A bad fingering is often the reason for uncertain and inexact intonation, even in technically easy passages. This is the result of the awkward movements of the hand and fingers which are required by such fingerings. For example:

The fingering given above, which requires an extension of the second finger followed by the first finger crossing strings, gives the fingers no point of support, which is the reason for the uncertainty of intonation. The advantage of the following fingering:

is that by doing away with the unnecessary string crossing of the first finger, it gives a natural point of support for the precise movements of the fingers in the given hand position and thus makes for more accurate intonation.

However, the causes of uncertain intonation are not only bad fingering. It is well known that violinists make the same mistakes in intonation when playing the same passages in certain works. This is explained by the fact that such passages are not only technically *difficult*, but *awkward* as well. The shifts, jumps, and extensions which the left hand has to make in playing such passages are so foreign to the nature of the instrument and the natural position of the fingers, that no fingering will completely remove these difficulties, and all the efforts to overcome them do not always lead to the desired results. This is reflected not only in the uncertainty and inexactness of intonation, but also in the tone quality. For example, the following passage from the 'Recitative and Scherzo' of Kreisler is very difficult for intonation, owing to the lack of a point of support, the quick changes of position, the sound of the open E string, and the finger extensions:

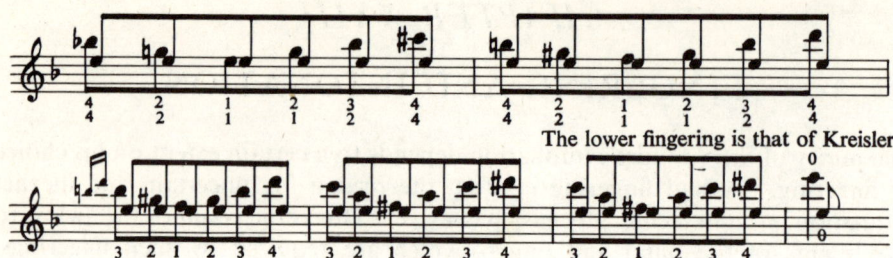

The lower fingering is that of Kreisler

The examples given below also contain a number of difficulties and awkward features, as a result of which they usually sound poor:

The reason for the difficulty in securing good intonation in many modern works is that the technical foundation of the violinist is based mainly on the study of the virtuoso violin repertoire, the limited harmonic range of which is well known. It is natural that having easily overcome the difficulties of passages based on tonic-dominant harmonies, the violinist should experience difficulties in playing whole-tone scales or complicated combinations of double stops, chords, and harmonic progressions. The question is not so much one of the violinist's fingers, which are sufficiently developed, but of his ear, which has been trained and developed on completely different progressions and combinations of notes, resulting in the lack of a sufficiently developed aural faculty. The development of good intonation is helped by the use of rational fingering, but this demands certain technical skills which are at times strange for the violinist who has been brought up on different types of fingering and has been used to different positions and movements of the fingers on the finger-board.

The uncritical learning of fingering in the early stages of playing leads to the pupil later feeling a certain awkwardness in using new rational fingering methods. It is therefore essential to introduce systematically into early teaching practice new kinds of movements and positions of the fingers on the finger-board and enharmonic changes of intervals, and to insist on the use of the normally avoided even-numbered positions and the half position.

Rubinstein's comment on pianists' reluctance to use the thumb on the black keys offers an instructive parallel. Rubinstein pointed out that 'if one is afraid of putting the thumb on the black keys, then in many pieces of the modern repertoire one is bound to come up against considerable difficulties (regarding the choice of fingering) at every step; one should therefore get used to the black keys as soon as possible (that is, get used to fingerings in which the thumb is naturally used on the black keys).'[1]

---

[1] *The lectures of Hans von Bülow*, compiled by Theodore Pfeiffer from the 4th German edition, with remarks by A. Bukhovtsev (Moscow, 1896), p. 96.

CHAPTER XXIV

GLISSANDO AND PORTAMENTO

The violin is one of the so-called free tuning instruments, able to produce any shade and change of intonation on any note. This tuning is a constant source of expressiveness in violin playing, a means of bringing out the artistic individuality of the violinist. The splendid words of B. V. Asafiev, that the performing art is a creative process as far as intonation is concerned, can be applied without qualification to the playing of the violinist.[1]

This statement of Asafiev has been confirmed by N. A. Garbuzov. By the scientific analysis of performances of the same work by different violinists, he has established the existence of individual styles of intonation, as a result of which they each play the different intervals in an individual way according to their own emotional conception and interpretation of the music, without destroying the intonational integrity of the work. These intervals are so varied in pitch that one can only talk about the tuning of this or that performance, which, as Garbuzov says, is the result of the interaction of the zonal nature of musical hearing and the 'creative intonation' of the artist who is performing the melody.[2]

The question as to what extent fingering methods can be used as a means of achieving expressive playing on the violin is closely connected with one of the most debatable questions in violin teaching—the artistic significance of the glissando and the ways in which it should be performed.

The possibility and necessity of using the glissando in violin playing and its enormous significance as a means of achieving expressiveness is beyond question. This is confirmed not only by the artistic practice of the most famous violinists, but also by the scientific research of modern scholars. In one such work, devoted to the study of intonation in practical musical performance on the basis of analysing recordings of violinists, the author makes a number of scientific conclusions which have a direct bearing on the question we are discussing.

He writes: 'In a melody, apart from the musical notes written by the composer, there are certain joins—the movements from one note to another, which occupy, it is true, only a minute amount of time (on average about 0.05 to 0.2 seconds). These joins between notes are occupied either with ascending or descending sounds or with a kind of pause, which is also filled with sound of some sort. In an artistic performance of a musical work we do not notice these joins and do not consider them as a separate melodic element. It follows that they are an integral part of the melody, and it would not be an exaggeration to say that the way in which the performer moves from sound to sound (the time taken in moving, the extent of the glissando, etc.) is one of the most important factors in artistic performance, on the same level as the modification of intervals, which we discussed earlier, and the type of vibrato, which we will talk about later.'[3]

By glissando is generally understood the sliding from one note to another. On the violin there are in practice two types of such sliding. For example:

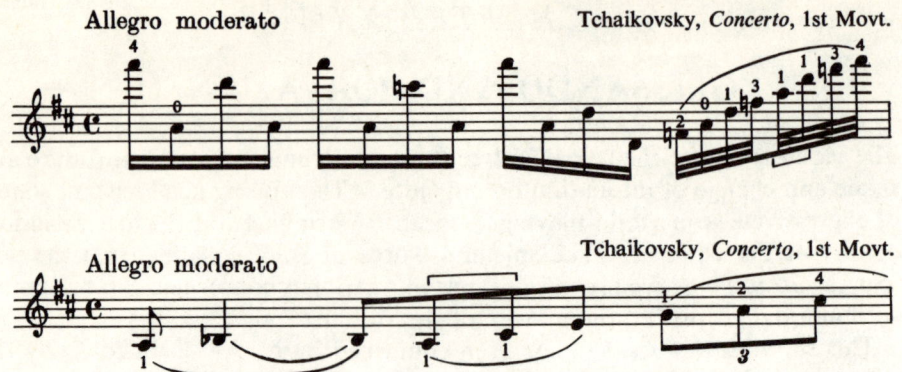

In the first case, the sliding is an essential *auxiliary device* facilitating the position change; in the second, it is *a means of increasing the expressiveness of the sound*. This accounts for the basic difference both in the character of the slide and the means of its execution. In the first case, the quicker and less obtrusive the slide the better (this should be noted by all violinists). In the second, the slide can be relatively quicker or slower or even not used at all, depending on the individual taste of the performer.

Flesch, in his book *The Art of Violin Playing*, is conscious of this distinction, and suggests that we establish the following more accurate terminology—the fast slide (in technical passages) to be called a glissando, and the slower, more expressive slide used in cantilena to be called *portamento*.

This distinction to a large extent corresponds to the different character of these movements, and underlines the connection between the portamento used in instrumental cantilena and the portamento used in vocal performance.

The question of the expressive slide—portamento—is considerably more complicated than that of the auxiliary fast slide—the glissando.

The portamento is a slow sliding movement. Its use as a means of combining two sounds in an expressive cantabile style depends on the individual, but cannot, nevertheless, be used indiscriminately. It should always be subject to the *musical content* of the piece or extract being performed. It should *intensify the expressiveness* and *underline the significance* of those notes which in the given musical phrase are the most important.

In the definition of Bériot which we have already quoted, it was stated: 'The fingering used by different virtuosi in melodic passages is an important means of expression; it is used for binding the sounds together and for imitating the inflexions of the human voice. It varies from performer to performer according to the sentiment he wishes to express, but at the same time is a *stumbling-block for many and its misuse can easily lead to unwholesome excess*.'

In his remark that 'in fingering cantabile melodies' the misuse of melodic fingering 'can easily lead to unwholesome excess' Bériot had in mind the misuse of portamento.

The following kinds of portamento are possible:

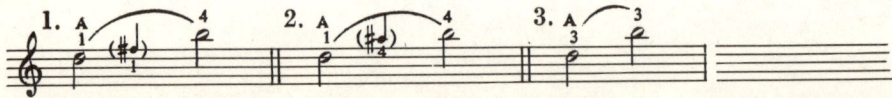

In the first case, the slide is made by the finger taking the first note, and the higher note is taken by a different finger.

In the second, the slide is made basically by the finger taking the higher note.

In the third, the slide is made and both notes taken by the same finger.

From an artistic point of view, the question as to which of these various methods of portamento to use is determined by the interpretation of the given musical passage and the individual taste of the performer, as each of these methods produces its own particular characteristic sound. Thus according to which of these methods he chooses, the violinist can give different shades of sound to the same musical phrase.

The first method, in which the slide is made by the finger taking the *lower* note, with the higher note taken by a different finger, without preparation, produces a clear, well-defined, and rather objective sound.

The second, in which the slide (produced basically by one finger) is linked with the final note, which is not arrived at immediately but with the finger gradually approaching (sliding towards) it, produces a more sensual, soft and rather subjective sound.

The third, which is produced by the direct slide of the same finger from one note to the other, gives a particular expressiveness to the sound, similar to the expressive effect of portamento in the human voice.

The art of combining sounds in cantabile passages consists in the artistic combination and variation of these three types of portamento. The endless fine shades of sound which can be achieved in this way at times make them indistinguishable one from the other.

One must pay attention to the question of whether the portamento should be played in one box (i.e. legato) or whether the change of bow should coincide with the position change, and also to the importance of the various kinds of bowing in playing portamento.

In playing separate bows, it is essential to make the portamento (whatever type is used) coincide with the change of bow. In such cases one must take into account the following :

In the first type of portamento, the change of bow should coincide with the upper note (after the auxiliary note) :

In the second type, the opposite is the case ; the auxiliary note is taken with the new bow for the whole of the slide :

In the third type, as with the first, the slide takes place on the bow taking the initial note :

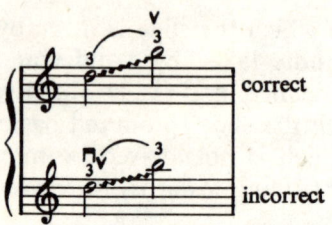

Portamento on an open string in legato bowing is taken :

in separate bows :

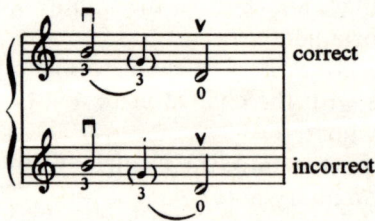

For downward portamenti on one string :

on two strings :

Emphasizing the portamento by using various kinds of accents with the bow gives the cantilena a declamatory character. In this connection the portamento used by Kreisler, which was so widely imitated at the time, is particularly characteristic. The Kreisler portamento is based mainly on the *sliding of one finger*. It is not smooth and flowing, but is emphasized by the simultaneous pressure of the finger of the left hand with a particular kind of accent with the bow on the *final point of the slide*. The Kreisler portamento is not the classical portamento, which is a means of smoothly connecting two sounds, but a kind of pathetic accent, rather elevated and affected. For example:

Of quite a different style is the portamento of Oistrakh, whose playing is characterized by the use of a smooth downward portamento in cantilena. This gives a particularly lyrical and sincere quality to his playing. For example:

At the present time it is generally accepted that one should not use several portamenti in succession over short distances, either up or down. For example:

Naturally, we do not mean to refer to those instances where the composer indicates this, as for example:

It is also not recommended to use several portamenti in succession with the same finger, although it should be added that in the first half of the 19th century many great violinists (Paganini, Spohr, Lvov, and others) often did so. For example:

The use of portamento, as we have pointed out, belongs entirely to the realm of the interpretation of a musical work, to the style of its performance. If for the purely technical side of violin playing there exist comparatively objective principles for so-called correct playing, which have been reached as a result of the experience of a long period of development in violin technique, we cannot say the same as regards artistic interpretation, which belongs entirely to the field of aesthetics.

The musical art of each age, which is conditioned by social factors, develops and acquires new characteristic modes of expression. The contemporary art of musical performance, which is feeling the need for new modes of expression, in many ways distinct from those characteristic of the musical performing practice of past times, is gradually bringing into practice these new modes of artistic expression, which should be carefully studied by violinists.

[1] B. V. Asafiev (Igor Glebov), *Musical form as a process*, Book 2, ' Intonation ' (Moscow/Leningrad, 1947), p. 91.
[2] N. A. Garbuzov, *The zonal nature of musical hearing* (Moscow/Leningrad), 1950. As given in K. Mostras, *Intonation on the violin*.
[3] A. V. Rabinovich, *The oscillographic method of analysing melody* (Moscow/Leningrad, 1932), p. 29.

CHAPTER XXV
CANTILENA AND TONE QUALITY

In cantilena, fingering is indissolubly linked with phrasing as a mode of artistic expressiveness. The choice of fingering for cantilena passages should in the first instance be determined by the length of phrases and the timbre and character of the sound required by the content of the melody. From a technical point of view, phrasing consists primarily in the correct movement of the bow, and in the choice of a rational fingering on the basis of the rhythm and dynamic of the given phrase. Incorrect fingering, like incorrect bowing, destroys the overall effect of an artistic phrase and leads to the distortion of the musical sense of the work performed.

If it is necessary in technical passages to choose a convenient fingering for facilitating execution, allowing one to overcome the difficulties of quick shifts, jumps and extensions, in cantilena (at slower tempi) it is possible to choose a fingering which allows a greater number of shifts with the aim of increasing expressiveness. Thus a fingering which is suitable for cantilena at a slow tempo may be unsuitable for the same passage at a fast tempo. For example:

The sound of the violin is the sound of its strings. Each of the four strings, which has its own particular timbre, has in addition various shades of tone quality in its different registers. Therefore:

(1) The choice of string should be in accordance with the character of the melody and the nuances required:

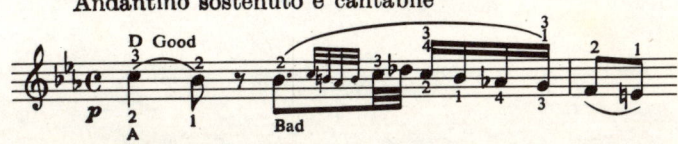

In the above example the sound of the D string in piano is more suited to the character of the melody than the open and sharper sound of the A string.

(2) In choosing the fingering for a melodic phrase, one should aim at preserving uniformity of timbre by playing the phrase as far as possible on one string:

A change of string in such cases should be in accordance with the general structure of the given melody:

(3) The musical sense of a melodic fragment often requires the avoidance of what is in the context an unnecessary portamento and instead the use of a finger *extension*:

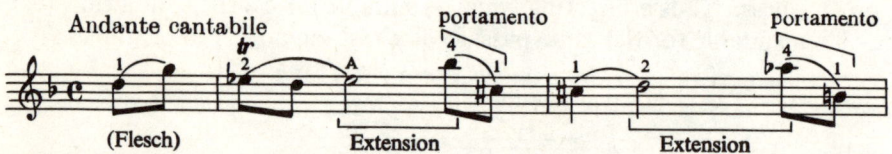

In the example given above, the portamento from the lower note to the higher is illogical and destroys the musical sense of the phrase.

(4) The repetition of a musical phrase normally implies a change of nuance and fingering, which generally takes the form of using different strings for the repetition. This is necessary in order to give the repetition more variety so as to underline its significance:

(5) When a single note is repeated in a melody, a *change* of finger on that note, changing its timbre, increases its expressiveness:

(6) The use of the fourth finger in cantilena should be limited, as it does not always lead to good tone : (*a*) in the very high positions, (*b*) in places requiring great strength and richness of tone (particularly on the G string). The reasons for the comparatively poor sound in certain cases when using the fourth finger are : (*a*) its comparative physical weakness, (*b*) the limitation of the extent of vibrato possible, (*c*) its unreliability in the higher positions :

Kreisler excludes the use of the fourth finger in expressive cantabile passages, using a slide of a different finger instead. For example :

(7) We have already considered the various possibilities of using natural harmonics in violin playing in Chapter XX. The use of natural harmonics (chiefly E, A, D, G) at various octaves in cantilena gives a soft and expressive sound, especially in combination with portamento in pianissimo, piano and mezzo-forte. This can be used in the following cases :

(*a*) In phrases, the musical sense of which requires a certain softness and limpidity of texture :

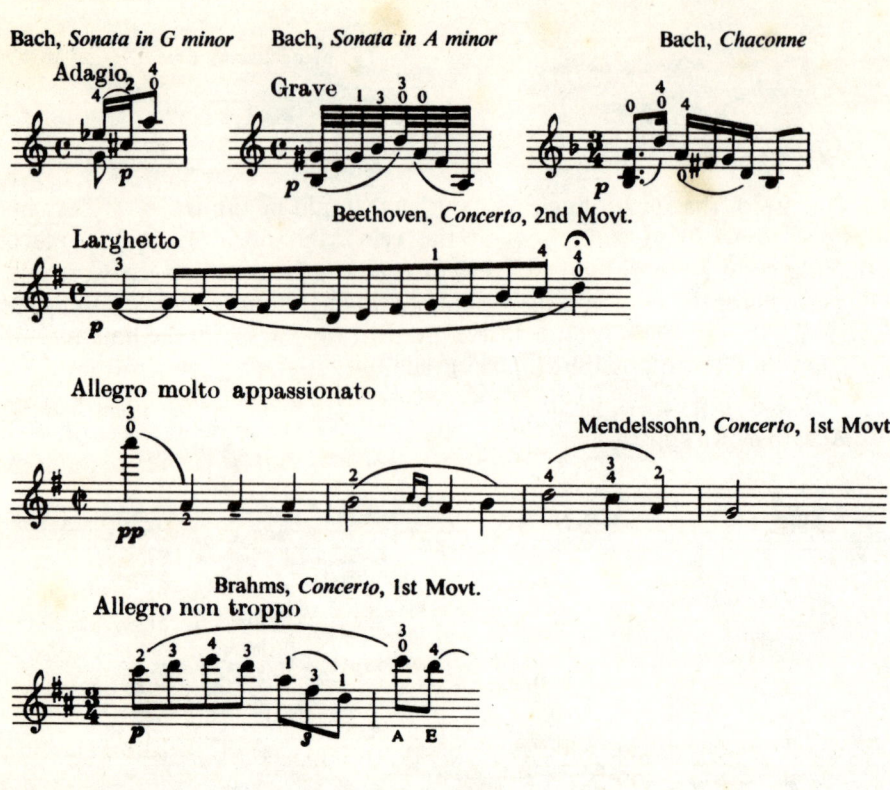

(b) In passages of a refined and graceful character:

CONCLUSION

The expressive means used by the performer are basically determined by his artistic intentions, and in this sense the *technique* of the violinist cannot be separated from his *interpretation*. The means of producing the sound, the type of vibrato, the style of bowing, phrasing, fingering, etc.—the use of all these is entirely determined by the style of the performance.

For any one style of musical performance there exists its own particular complex of technical devices which are in a manner of speaking the technique of that style. *Technical considerations spring from artistic considerations, and have no absolute significance.*

From this it will be seen that the present book should be considered as a guide, which may help the violinist to find his way in the general question of the choice of fingering, but by no means as a collection of universal rules and unchangeable propositions.

The author's own artistic views and convictions have forced him to criticize those fingering methods which he considers have outlived their usefulness, and similarly to discuss certain factors to which insufficient attention has been paid in the past. This has inevitably led to the laying down of general principles and propositions concerning the systematization of fingering devices and the establishment of a system of rational fingering which in many respects cuts across old habits and traditions.

If we consider the historical development of the technique of playing musical instruments, we can observe a clearly defined tendency for technical methods of playing to become similar. The history of music gives a number of examples of such simplification, which opened up new artistic possibilities for both composers and performers.

If we consider the development of violin fingering methods in this light, we can observe that such simplifications, which were connected with the elimination of unnecessary movements in the left hand, were the result of using hitherto undeveloped technical devices—the contracted position of the fingers, which led to the maximum use of the fourth finger and the half-position, the concept of the position as having an extent of a fourth to a fifth, and the use of the even-numbered positions. Rational fingering based on these methods is a new and important resource for the technique of the left hand, characteristic for the modern stage of the development of the art of violin playing.

If the elements of dynamics and bowing belong to the technique of the *right hand*, the timbre of the instrument is basically a question of *left hand* technique—the type of vibrato, the use of portamento, position playing—all connected with the choice of fingering.

Fingering, as an element of artistic performance, is indivisible from tone-colour; therefore *a different fingering means a different tone-colour*.

The revealing of the intellectual and emotional content of a musical work through the use of all the rich resources of tone-colour is one of the most important tasks which face the violinist.

INDEX OF MUSIC EXAMPLES
Compiled by Kelvin Mason
Abbreviations: m, movement; /, arranger

ARENSKY Concerto: 116
BACH, J. S. Partita I (Sarabande) 89
 Partita II (Chaconne) 31, 85, 88, 128
 Partita III (Gigue) 69; (Loure) 85; (Prelude) 66, 88, 95, 96
 Sonata I (Adagio) 89, 128; (Fugue) 31; (Presto) 91; (Siciliano) 79, 85, 89
 Sonata II (Andante) 89; (Fugue) 78, 85, 89, 90; (Grave) 128
 Sonata III (Fugue) 90
BACH/WILHELMJ Air for the G string 127
BACH, W. F./KREISLER Grave 123, 127
BAZZINI Dance of the Elves 42
BEETHOVEN Concerto (1m) 43, 66, 80, 81, 92, 98, 103, 105, 117; (3m) 43, 49, 50, 86, 91, 103
 Sonata Op. 24 (2m) 126; (4m) 92
 Sonata Op. 30, No. 2 (1m) 29, 49, 118; (2m) 115
 Sonata Op. 30, No. 3 (3m) 97
 Sonata Op. 47 (1m) 66, 75, 118
BÉRIOT Method Op. 102 [1858] 26, 53, 61
BEZEKIRSKY Short Historical Survey . . . [1913] 31
BIZET/SARASATE Carmen Fantasy 69, 70, 79, 105
BOUCHER My Caprice 42
BRAHMS Concerto (1m) 44, 45, 46, 68, 69, 72, 85, 88, 89, 127, 128; (3m) 30, 43, 46, 58, 78, 82
BRUCH Concerto in G minor (3m) 44
CAMPAGNOLI New Method [1791] 52
CHAUSSON Poème 79
CHOPIN/SARASATE Nocturne Op. 9, No. 2 123
CHOPIN/WILHELMJ Nocturne Op. 27, No. 2 78, 127
CONUS Concerto 102
CORELLI La Folia 127
CORRETTE L'École d'Orphée [1783] 3
DAVID Violin School [1863] 53
DONT Etudes Op. 35 (No. 1) 87
 Etudes Op. 37 (No. 3) 72
ERNST Concerto 74
 Etudes (No. 6) 109
FRANCK Sonata (2m) 98
FRANCOEUR Sonata No. 8 (Allegro) 89
GEMINIANI Art of Playing on the Violin [1739] 4, 5, 51
GERHARD, J. Wolff
 Tanz: Bei mir mein Herz [1613] 2
GLAZUNOV Concerto 36, 64, 75, 78, 79, 86
GOLDMARK Concerto (1m) 42
GOUNOD/WIENIAWSKI Faust Fantasy 44, 104
GUHR Paganini's Art of Playing the Violin [1829] 11
HANDEL Sonata in D (2m) 91
HUBAY Zephyr 104
JAROSY, Albert New Theory of Fingering [1922] 55
JOACHIM & MOSER Violin School [1905] 25, 53 54, 55, 56
KABALEVSKY Concerto (1m) 49; (2m) 64; (3m) 31, 91, 123
KHACHATURIAN Concerto (1m) 45
KHANDOSHKIN Russian Songs with Variations 9, 10
 Sonata in D (1m) 88, 89
KREISLER Allegretto 128
 Caprice Viennois 75
 Praeludium and Allegro 96, 99
 Précieuse, La 128
 Recitativo and Scherzo Caprice 117
 Siciliano and Rigaudon 72, 93, 97
 Variations on a Theme of Corelli: 91
L'ABBÉ, Jos. B. Les Principes du violon [1761] 8
LALO Symphonie espagnole (1m) 42, 63, 110, 115; (4m) 44; (5m) 45, 49

LECLAIR Sonata Op. 12, No. 1 (Allegro) 90
LIAPUNOV, Sergei Concerto 46, 68, 81, 101, 116
LOCATELLI Art of the Violin [1733] 4
LVOV, Alexis Caprices (No. 5) 124
MENDELSSOHN-BARTHOLDY, Felix Concerto (1m) 46, 58, 69, 72, 126, 127, 128; (2m) 125, 127; (3m) 30, 31, 48, 50, 58, 67, 94, 104
MERCK, Daniel A Short Treatise of Instrumental Music [1695] 3, 51
MOZART, Leopold Violin School [1756]: 5, 6, 7, 8, 52
MOZART, W. A. Concerto No. 4 (1m) 42; (2m) 103, 126
 Concerto No. 6 (1m) 49, 50, 63
 Sonata No. 10 in B flat (1m) 93; (2m) 125
NARDINI Concerto in E minor (2m) 126
OISTRAKH, David Cadenza for Khachaturian Concerto 100
PAGANINI Caprices, Op. 1 (No. 1) 74; (No. 4) 74, 89; (No. 5) 36, 69; (No. 9) 44, 58; (No. 13) 76; (No. 17) 58, 63, 99; (No. 20) 81; (No. 21) 11; (No. 24) 64, 69, 82, 94
 Concerto in D (1m) 75
 Perpetual Motion 100
PAGANINI/KREISLER Campanella, La 43, 73, 103, 109
 Witches' Dance 37, 68, 108
PLAKSIN, M. G. Contracted Fingering [1933] 15
POPPER/AUER Spinning Song 64
RAKOV, Nicholas Concerto (1m) 123
RIMSKY-KORSAKOV Fantasy on Russian Themes 103
ROIERE, K. Sonata No. 3 (Minuet) 90
ROSSINI/ERNST Othello Fantasy 79
SAINT-SAËNS Concerto in B minor (1m) 44, 46; (3m) 92
 Introduction and Rondo Capriccioso 45, 67, 100
SARASATE Zapateado 58, 108
SCHUBERT, François (of Dresden) Bee, The 45
SCOTT/KREISLER Lotus Land 103
SCRIABIN/SZIGETI Etude in Thirds 75
ŠEVČÍK School of Violin Technique, Op. 1, Part 3 [1883] 71
SPOHR Concerto No. 9 (1m) 60, 61
 Concerto No. 10 (2m) 124
SZYMANOWSKI Concerto (cadenza) 45, 123
TANEIEV, Alexander Concert Suite (Prelude) 45
TARGONSKY, Y. B. Harmonics of String Instruments [1936] 109
TARTINI Sonata, 'Devil's Trill' (1m) 37, 126
TCHAIKOVSKY Concerto (1m) 36, 46, 64, 95, 104, 110, 120; (2m) 126, 128; (3m) 49
TESSARINI, Carlo New Method [1762] 51
VIEUXTEMPS Concerto No. 2 (1m) 78
 Concerto No. 4 (1m) 110
 Fantasia appassionata 49
VIOTTI Concerto No. 23 (1m) 29, 31, 57, 96, 97
VITALI Chaconne 63
VIVALDI Concerto in A minor (1m) 31
WAGNER/WILHELMJ Romance (Albumleaf) 68
WASSMANN, C. Discoveries Promoting Ease and Development of Violin Technique [1885] 55
WIENIAWSKI Concerto No. 2 (1m) 62; (3m) 43, 98, 104
 Obertass 102
 Polonaise in A 96, 103
 Scherzo tarantelle 92
YSAŸE Sonata Op. 27, No. 6 35